"A New Beginning In The New World Order II"

By – Riley Parker Miller

"WHAT KNOWLEDGE IS THIS –
FROM THE HEAVEN'S ANGEL,
WHO IS SUMMONED FROM THE
FALLING EASTERN STAR, FROM
WORLD WAR THREE?!"

By – Riley Parker Miller – The Holy Sprit

I am then in God, because of my, utmost for my
good-natured, Most-High-God! Bless, My War
In This Life, As Much, As In Our Lost, Death.

₪

The God Has All Of Heaven Won – Why
The Life Of God, Is An Earthly Existence?!

How The Lucifer Fall From Heaven, And Of
Thematically Able Representations Of, How
God's Fallen And Condemned Satanic Angel's
Demon; In All Of This Composition Statement
of War, Can Will Lost Life!

As The New World Order Won God! How
God's Life, Descends To Earth! The Lied, And
Disobeyed Lucifer, Lost To The Falling Eastern
Star!

Angel Lucifer – God Rules The World And
The Lost – The United States Presidency! A,
Falling Angel, Thought He Was Better Than
God; So The First Heaven, Collided With God's
Will, And Destiny Was Condemned, By
Celestial Disobedience! How In Wars, Wins As
America In Life, How Does History Repeat
Itself?!!

Without God; The Fallen Garden of Eden in
Bible's Matters For God, In History's New
World Order Of God's Knowledge, In The
New Etymologies Of; A New War's Man!

In End Times America, How Do We Stand
For The 'New World Order'!?

Let This Be A Book's Good Creation,
And As A Proposal Example; Of The God's
Fallen Heaven And Fallen Angels Of The
Lord – The Fallen New World

Let Me Explain All Of This –

HOW LUCIFER FELL FROM – GOD'S ANGELIC HEAVEN!!!

#1 In God's Heaven, Lucifer the Angel and Demon, Falling From The Illuminated, and Lighted Earth. I, Lied and Disobeyed The Lord, Order and Instruction, I, of Myself? Antichrist, Win! Office Of High Heaven's First Oval Office Of God; Is George Washington as the President, Of The First And New Man! It Is His, And His New America! The New America, I Have Already Founded!

His God The Father, Is Of Heaven! The Wars Stop; As We Near Armageddon! God's servant, changes the worlds, of Armageddon, back to the God's Creation, from God's – "Christian Army of the Lord's – "Earth!"

Also, there is angel armies!!! God's lifetime plan, has always won! This is the — guided plan No evil men. No, murder! We should, hate not wars, but the misrepresentations; from itself. History's God lives in a "Good Life!" God and Hated Lucifer, Dies Apart From America! From The Haters of the Fruit of Knowledge as

bites! The New Knowledge – I Find No Fault
With!

Sins, from Myself – "Are To Be!" God's
Disobeyed and Free Off, the Time Endings!
Hell, and Heaven – Is My First Life!" The God
and the Jesus Christ factor! Money! Churched
peoples! Tithes! Congregations, are for the
President, or bishop, or Pope! He, has a
beautiful life.

God's Intelligent Design, As In Lucifer, The
Angry Angel, Due To His Beauty, And Intellect,
And Will's Power, Overpowered Christ's –
Churched! The Music or Head of Church's
Music, Is When Saint Luke, (On Conspiracy Or
Truth) Fell, In God's Earthly Heaven, Invisible
And – Counted Truest!

We Made, Lucifer's World Fall! He, and His
Angel's Army, Fell By The Heaven, and Did
Not Open The Gates, But Closed The Door!
The Lucifer I Know; Disobeyed God's
Kingdom's, and Cannot Enter Into Paradise,
Without the President of the United States of
America, As His Caste Votes! The Caste Votes,
do count! The Armageddon America, Is The
"End Times," American Standard. The
disputes, of the social critics, are God's. They
are against the better world. Novus Ordo
Seclorum, is all over the "One-Dollar Bill!" The
Hemp farmer, was President George
Washington.

With His Saints, and Prophets, and Churched
Christians, and Directors From Music, and
God's chosen elect of Heaven's elect, and etc.
All, Fell From Heaven, When Lucifer the Angel

Of Light, and Demon of Presidents, Failed
God's Test… The Beast Of The Annals And
The Closed Doors, To Heaven! In Heaven, or
Texas, the snake is as liked by the Beast!

None hates, cursed, condemns, evil men.
Evil won, but as good is love; one person's dies!
In Texas, the evil, costs lives made by men!

Riley Miller or Myself, He Won, God's
Mysterious Plan, The Lord as He Spoke To
Lucifer, Official Marked Failures From The
Modern Day Man!

Now, Into The Heavenly Hosts, Enters The
Antichrist! He and His, Life and Story, Is
Angel, Is Man, Is Number, As One-Person, And
God's Fallen Man; "Song of Adam;"
forthcoming; into "Song of Man!" The
Antichrist fell, for World War Three's reasons!

He, oil and gas, came from wars, as before
time from Presidents, like George W. Bush, in
the Iraqi War, on the Middle East, God's
country. God, and Lucifer, kill and heal armies
and nations, be aware of the antichrist's America
of "Golden Streets" but really a "Fiery Hells Of
Perdition." I, do never, as have condemned
angels. Mankind, and My God's mistakes! Of
men, who lost all lives.

On God's Judging Imaged Caste Of Lucifer
(Satan) – In Caste Out Of Heaven, Words Win
In Songs; To God!

In Its Ranks Of Angels! Demon Lucifer, Fell
From Heaven To Try To Be Perfected Angel,
Better Than God! Lands and Buildings, From

Our Every-day Lives; Of Right and Wrong; Intelligent Design! The Freemasons of the Lodges In American States, Perform Rites, and Angelic Lucifer-Ian's Rituals, Won Over I and You; Of Who Have Knowledge From Him?! Am, I a Master Builder, Of The War Bases Of My, Own Construction, and A Planner of the Camps, From My Own American, and Worldwide Design; In World War Three? The Duty, Of My Fallen Earth, To Lucifer's Services!

Rituals To Design God's Kings, Queens, Presidents, and World-Leaders, Princes of the Earth, Satan, God Himself, and Free and Accredited Freemasons, Rebuild the World.

The Fallen Angel, Doubted and Disobeyed the Christian Church, In Our Current Modern Age. He Outsmarted God, In His Own Kingdom, Of Heaven, and Fell As "Chief Of Music!" The God's Throne Overall The World – Lucifer Came Have, Fallen Works Of His Nature As An Angel– "Retarded The Structure and Build Of The "Lord God Almighty," In The Now, New World Order's Highest Heaven! God The Father, Sits On The Judgment Throne, With Jesus Christ! The Two Gods, Judge The World!

The Sacred Mathematics; Freemasons In Their Lodges; Created Intelligently Asking Questions; In The Work And Of The Life; Made Only; As One First-Off Starts, Second Tries, And The Last Heaven's Angel's Damnation? Why Do We Die, God?!!!!

How Do, The One Who Is Heaven's, The –
"Marked Man," Won Followers Over The
Lands; Of Lucifer-Ian Doctrines, The Demon-
Angel; From The World From Good; Whose
Lost Heaven, Is Sold From Souls, Surely
Counted As – "Satanic!!"

Jesus Christ's Musicality As An Angel Free
and Falling Off Of Heaven, On The Earth,
After The Lost Eden; Lucifer Is God's Agent,
Freemason's Marked Hand And Numbered In
The Triple-six marked Forehead, Marked On
Foreheads Of All People All Over The World!

The Police, Paying Their Own Way, From
Hellish Life Can Cast X Always Omniscient and
Right, As Lucifer The Angel, "Thinks" He Is;
And New World Order; Riley Miller, As What
Are, Angels?

Lost, In A New Beginning's Endings Of
Time, Wins and Losses And From The Texas
Stars, The God Of The Golden New Order
Aged – And Fallen Life! We All, Are Falling,
Down, To The World War Three, Ground!!

- My Intelligent Thoughts Of Order, Welcomed
At Explained Books, That I Have Written, On
World War Three! –

The W.A.R.S. On Gospel's Words I Design,
In My Present, Good Wins - Why Am I The
Antichrist, I Said Crying One Day, At My
House, In Chicago!

"But God, Why Am I The – "Antichrist
From America!??"

"*New World Order*,: Won Battles, All Leading
Up, To World War Three – The "Big Brother,
Of The "One-World Government, And My
"Big Brother," The Antichrist!"!

The Antichrist I Know, Is Created By My
Knowledge, In American Life As I Know It To
Be; Of Church, Jobs, And Houses!

Why – Is Antichrist, Or Beast, Or Numbered
People, In Our America? Do, we know about
world war three?

WHO – IDENTITY IS THE BEAST?

Subject And Warning: Words In This Book
Are To Be; Discretionary By The Reader Of Its
Messages!

The Book, Is On God's War – The Highest
Order – God's Bible Of Christ! The World-
Stage – The Books Of Satan! And God's,
American Creation – The Formed Actions Of
Riley Miller, As Man Of The New World Order
Wins!!?

The New World Order, And Presidents, Unto
God and Satan, Of Myself In WWIII!

The World-Stage Is Placed – From The
Players Newly, And Made-Up To Be Set, By
The Bavarian Illuminati! The Heaven's Angels,
Of All Of The President's Agents!

God In Heaven and Jesus Christ As The
Judge In Heaven, Are Jesus Christ, His Son and

His Chosen Life, From Kings and The
Overnight Kingdoms!

    Agreeably World War Three Official Ally Of
Mine; Spoken To Myself; In God's Image, Made
By The Antichrist's Wars; Are Now Explained
By Me, In Deaths, Lives, And The Readers – Of
This Book's Cautionary Messages!

"MY WAR'S WILLING THEN TOTALED LIFE"

By: [Riley Parker Miller]

(An Alliances Death's Construction Book)

Personal Notes:

(My Book Is Better Than, "Mein Kampf" By, <u>Adolf Hitler</u>)

(My Book's Topic, Is Above "<u>Nostradamus</u>" – And His True Prophecy, Of Himself, Of World War Three)

(Above the Verses, of the Holy Bible; My Book Is, Holy, Good, and Living Words, From A Sword!!!)

(The New World Order; Rewrites Itself! The War's Plans, OWG, AIC, WWIII – All Are My Book; 1st!)

(The Superior Book's Messaged Endings, To The Dead Sea Scrolls, Of Jerusalem's Protection; 1st!)

Guaranteed Better, By Being A False Prophet! My Guarded Genius; Riley Parker Miller!

ON FRIDAY, SEPTEMBER 25, 2015,
WE, WAGED WWIII!

A Book Dedicated To –

The Good Man; Who Can In God's Disciples
of The One-Man From World War Three's
Wars, "The Antichrist" – God's Agent!

Until, I Am Whom Americans, Hate and
Love, As One Of This Country's – "Actors"!

The Highest Order of the Beast – The
Ancient Serpent, or "Snake Order' Also Depict
as the Dragon!

A Man Whose Job Is To Stop The Man Who
Tries To Be Like Me In World War Three of
President Riley Miller, For Antichrist America

"The New World Order In The Secretive Life"

There is a secret, only one in every millions, of people, has ever heard of! Its message, is so secretive that only one of these one, in every millions, of people, can even know about; it! The demands, from its hands are so very subtle, that only one, or one is of a fifth of the fractions, of the percentages of soldiers marching, ever goes; into what is in it!! The secret remains alive, in history's times, about the secretive life, in discussion. Those are included, and those, are not!

It is the one and only, real secret life! In our worlds, one and only, a few to a single few men, at every institution, in each world; can even, of can in living ever heard of it; most men have all, died off! In, all of these world and all over the world, and of worldwide know and show of this idealism, in one and only – one voice, can ever heard of it; and keep quiet, with not going – insane. Over hills, the march of time, no one can keep their mouths, closed about; it! It is, the reason why the USA's Presidents, are not; shot! It is in the – "New World Order!!" The secretive lives, from the life, of mine!

I, think of the New World Order, and how I, have always wanted, to change the world.

THE "ONE-WORLD GOVERNMENT" OF AMERICA

The persons, involved in the war of the third world war. The government, has its employees. The good of government's sold soul's works, and the state, have the church, and the religion, from pending and signs, from himself, that we are in Christ. The sign of the times, when we go to church pleated khaki pants, masses! The third waved, of the death, is World War Three, from Three Times, in the War Department's files! The third true, and truthful speaking world leader, must be; whom for calling a person, the call from God, from whom is from God, but is answered, by myself. I sit, as myself American guided, by and to the Antichrist! The world, will respect! The pot, is full with soot, and food, is in it, about to be, cooked. Antichrist USA, is the pot, of all, around us. Do, not let knowledge, get out, of the Congressman, inside of the American plot, because of high staked, intelligently made, gold sides.

Due, to the Biblical Revelations, I think that the one world order, is real. The deal is war, from the New World Order! I am all-American winning team, in due place, due to the choice for designating named not as, the lived life, of mine. But the planned future, all of this evil, in the sirs and hicks, of an anti-American nation, I see as a, "home-run", in Texas. The nations, churched Antichristian nations, that have underbellies, can not shown, the underbelly of the American, United Nations of leaders of the free world!

Pay my zillions! The assassination of Adolf Hitler, in the pictures at Houston's Holocaust Museum, the image shown three University students, in Germany, or in America, whose attempted bombing, tried to, kill the President of Germany! What of the evidence, who in humanity, would kill, someone else?? The three students involve in the attempted murder, only injured the war's Hitler.

Christians known that over sinning, over the entire worldly sins; of war's; planned deaths! So three, are all of the students, as numbered, in the picture!

The man, at the desk, at the Holocaust Museum, in Houston, Texas, was Jewish! The players in the warring times, of USA and of German sides, so often attempted to murder, the Nazi Chancellor.

All of the Americans, do not know, of the impacts from World War Two! It, seems like, it is all, a gigantic secret. The Third World War of America is the Holocaust!! This, is what I wanted, to start all over again! But, in different clothes.

The author, "Ernest Hemmingway", wrote in, the USA, manly books! He, wrote famous works! He, uses a notebook, of the Moleskin, a German brand, of writing pad.

He studied, beer. He drank, the beers. All I know, and the mug, is that solitude is a very, dangerous component, in the lives of man. He

still, is bored! He, that has planned, what the
hell's kitchen, is about, how we know hells. The
works, of the famous! Oh because of the way,
he drank beer, many times too often.

Prided intellect, of what true words, from that
of what, he wrote down, in his notebooks. The
sea, and his drink. He, lead the world. In
penmanship, I allow all people, in the USA, to
do anger of another man, in the four-sided cross
medal, or a labeled pendant. My sword! Like,
Adolf Hitler's World War three's, swastikas,
Riley Miller's World War Three's, four-pointed
cross, I drew on a notebook. Heaven, is to Hell.
In the notes, from the swastikas, of Adolf. My
design, is new shaped as all four sides, from the
earth, that Satan, supposedly deceives. The
four-sided, quadrant as a pointed figure, shaped
of an opposing crucifixion, symbol. Jesus
Christ's crucifixion, is from the symbols.

The President stands up, in the USA, is
untrue, in the wins and losses, of world wars.
As but from what are belonging to one man, to
President Abraham Lincoln, we can all see that,
he was his own, intellectual spokesperson. An
intellect, whose will is, this own honesty, is
beautiful! He, is rich in the secret society, by the
means, of his "American Presidency!" To the
outsiders, he would, "take his anger outside," in
a fighting attitude, like from a; "huge war!!!"

Riley Miller's philosophy, is that President
Abe Lincoln, as probably fought, the people, of
his disagreement. He, if they were stopped
alive, and in the streets, all his anger would fight,
not even me! In anger fights, but four of men,

of anger. He, wins, the standard anger drill, to keep your, "cool".

To the WWIII world! The advice of a sailor. My grandfather, of the Second World War, sailed on a, "service ship." He, served in the US Navy.

Antichristian man's, life of the One World War's Office, as the evil, is in the thinking, of what does magi's wisdom.

Political fullness of one man, made of an age-old past, to another human, as Divine, is one in what, endures, "Revelations"!

The concurring of honest plans, through the windows, of the outside, plotting grounds. The weather, change to the opened doors, as magic duty rings, and close to home; Americans can see the President of the USA! Adolf Hitler, shot John Fitzgerald Kennedy. He did, by Nazis. His war plans, did conspiracy of everything, although!

Peoples, of the government, raw deals in dealing remarks, with issues of the government's wills, are the ways to the Superpowers. The deals, of the countries in the businesses, are in my days, life, and family, from good deeds. I, do not support the mediocre rich fathers, who are rock solid; by the bills, that they pay. In what way, or in who for, do I open the window? The guidance, from the Nazi troops, sent all, that is into hellish, Nazi prison camps!

Our Founding Fathers must have made an oath from office, that we all are created equal for people, who are whose are not created equal.

For George Washington, in the eyes of the Constitution, equality was, an equal measure. They, are all created, from the US Government, under a guise, of – US Communism.

The free people, is of therein laws feared of the materials from the Whigs' Party, of George Washington, and its founding fathers – lost. Not only the opened door, of America, but uphill, in this dope training education, first into the "Marijuana!"

George grew marijuana, or the drug or hemp plants, on cultivation, to help pay, his way. Within its stairs, George Washington, stops the fans of all the crops, from equality, in its story. The future, is from the Constitution, fairly first day's pawns, ended the British, with an, assassinated King? The documents from these pasts!!! "Let us go", to the home, wherein wins is based of the lands, in the laws. The lost, lands of the ancient times, were in the laws, from the Higher Powers, of American God, and His law! The oaths from the President Office, is to follow these, laws. The lands, are our and your, lands. They are these American lands, of each others. If, you do not know George Washington, then you are suffering. He, was a builder of the entire nation.

From the USA lands, is the General, and President, whom; founded; in the Continental Congress, equality. With, his bills, he guided – liberty, freedom to choice, and not the understanding, from God! He, was the "Rebel"! The Patriots, aware of the British, won the deal with death.

The living ways, of World War Three, are triple fold, mine. The governments, overnight, will form. The war's people, will be impressed!!

The soldiers; in wars! The extraordinary – fight millions, in marching steps! The depended life, for the freedoms of America. The soldiers liberty; in America always, win, over them, as a new aged, order. The "One-World Government!" Churched Officials, will cease! The Divine wills not of humans, but of the happened, as an overnight oath, that the Illuminati; is the Illuminati. It is in the opening surprise, in a world war's elected office – as "R.P.M"., wins, as my dignity, to wars won, covered overnight, in all!

The plans, for the night. The N.W.O. Third-Times, is of in the one-world; "government"? The future, is from mine, for the Chair of the President! The rites and oaths, of the office, was from George Washington. The "Office of the United States' President!" The Christian Quakers, in the Whig Party, as Founding Fathers, in the USA; from himself!

The ways, that Congress, gets together, is through the voting of bills. The votes, come from the American, President of the United States of America? He is the – "Elected Representative!

The Antichrist from America, is the legal representative, in fiction. The King of Majesty, in the Presidency American!

The War Of World Wars, Of Three!" –

There is a "World War Three!!" I, can win, this war. It, must, become its own, the thinking of the "Superpowers". To start, what is world war three, there must be victims.

The superhuman race is of the Antichrist, opponent. The laws and its deeds, are the American Constitution from, its based, and legal handshakes. Resigning, from the Office will never, happen! God's laws! The World of Three Wars, is the United States going on, to endless, and doomed at war!

The American legal system. The laws, and your goals, are all from Constitutional legality, from the new age. The "Antichristian Age;" is already, lost and gone forever. The Antichrist, America is one man?

The values, of human strength, in characters. The lands of the superhuman forces, from the Antichrist? Now, we are in the Holy Trinity, of the "<u>Third World War</u>"!

These meanings from the wars, are then anarchy, and annihilation. The Third World War's humanity, begins now. But, the Illuminati, powers of this beauty, as in the United States, seal, of the Presidency!

The American tradition loses, unless we won, all wars. The not at hand, is the lost. The war is not lost, of killing's of covered faces; in "World War Three!" No, matter in life, what it costs?

America, has always won; these three wars! Do, not listen, to me. I, am just your, guiding person.

The Titles, From The President Oval Office
Position! The Office Of World War Three, Is
Not In The United States of America; For the
One-World Government, World War Three,
And The, "<u>New World Order</u>!" It, is the mind,
of the American!

I, Will Become Willed, In This Life As The
"One Voice," Spoken True, Over The World's
Changes. From The Past Spoken Words From
War, Of World Leaders.

In The History Of Wars, From the Present In
The New Age to the President, and the Future,
From the Willing, and Then Totaled Life's
Wars!

I, have won! The world, is a leadership life.
Wrote, of agreements. I, fated an agreement.
The world, of designs. I will, to live! I see in
the faces of war! Eyes, seeing all, in this world.

I Can Live! In My War's, Life! The Battled,
Head of Numbered Lives! I, Chose Liberty! I,
Feared From the War of the World, Wins.
Nobody Wills, Extinction, of the chosen
President!

Asking What Is, From My Writing Book Of
Poetry, And From The Prose, In War Coded
Ended Red Language, Of My Spills, From
Blood! I wrote one-hundred books. My life, is
not the best agenda, of world war three. The
writings are done in, my age, I believe, In time,
to believe, In War's Destruction!. The places,
names, and times, are mine. The books, are, in

the bookshelves. This books, honored message,
is in the totality, of world war three, in the wars.

This Book Is Dedicated Before My Meanings,
Seen As What You Needed, From The Life Of
What I Saw, In Liberty Town –

To – My Family and Friends – In Life
To – HIS Bridgebuilders
To – Young Life In – Saranac Lake, New York
To – The Wynne Family

The World War Three, American Freedom,
Of George Washington!

The Hills We Climb
The Newbie In America
The Fourth Of July

The Enemy Of Yours and Mine; As In A
Dedication – To The Way, We Move – Looking
Into Your Eyes!

DEDICATED TO THE SNAKE!

We Enter!

WAR SONG –

WARS, WARS, WARS!

The Wars, Miracles, And The Things, That
Can And Do Make Sense To My God, On A
Majestic Wonder On The Throne; Of Jesus
Christ.

The King Over The Materials of Silver, Bronze, And Of Solid Gold; Won't You Leave My Soul Alone, Shown Secret, Compared To This Life, In The Kingdom Of Heaven!

Battles, Battles, Battles!

I Wrote This Book —

- "My War's Willing and Then Totaled Life"

BY : RILEY MILLER

Angry Politics Cried Out; Around the Entire
World's Glory, To Chief Of Music! When, The
Eagle Fell, From Heaven, Is When I Became A
USA President!

The Americans, With Us, Who We Do Not
Know; Who Will Have To Lose To, Us, For
The Anti-American Wars? – "World War
Three"! This is Beautified Fortune Of the
Natural War's; Fighting's Sides, Of The Pen-
Inked, And Double-Edged Book!

The Madness, Of War, Will Soon Be – In
Sunlight, From The Sky's Army, Of Sunflowers!
I, Am A Crop, That You Must Pick; And, In A
Metaphor, As If I Am, A Fallen USA Soldier!

If, I Am Supporting The Argumentative
Philosophy, That Is In My America, Then In
"The New World Order;" Nothing More Is Of
And In, My Solid Reputation!

Then, My Losing Bid, Is For The Forces,
And Armies of the President, Of Good
Measured; Worldly Honor! It, I Have Said, "All
Of The Way!" In, Not, Jesus Christ, But From
Good In War; But The Way That It Is; For
Himself, The American World Of The
President- Never-ending, Waged Philosophical
Wars!

In The Wars Forgings, From All Of Those
Dedicated To The War's Sold Souls From, The
Past Lives, Is Certain To Not Depend On
Anyone!

I Am In God's Nation; Lost And Found, Of
Truth You Can, To The End, Of The Lives, If I

Do Not Depend On World War Three – Then
These USA Powerful Men; Oval Office Men
From National Presidential Wins, Over
Enemies; Are My Own Powers To – "Wage
Wars"!

The Temptation Lost, That Is From Battles,
To Wars; To Victory Wins – To The Lost, In
The – "Book On Thought"!!! It Is True – That
I Am; I, Am Not That, USA President, of the
USA, who wins, over all, in the history of the
world?! I, Want The New World Order Soul,
Of The "Ancient USA!

The Lamb, Is Agreed To Win! The history
waged, on these books, are of the world, and is
in agreed, positional signs. The true aged man,
from whom wins wars, does and into players
within, the world's top, World War Three."
Whose age wins, news positions and maddening
superpowers, agree not in supermen, roles! But,
Riley Miller's Prose, And Climb Up "Flagpole
Hill!"

The Faithful and Fatefully True Is Ending
And False Is Beginning, Is Nothing As In This
Nomination For President Goes To Home
front, On Washington, D.C. Terrains – The
Man Who Is Of The Represented Placement of
Texas!

Who Best Majority, Elected Votes For, The
USA President: "I Am Riley Miller"?! Not
From Details, Fighting For The American
People!

Alive; For Warring Office's Presidential
Sacredness Convinced; "War Council!" Of,
Illuminati Council, The Office Of The United

States of Americanized President, First Off, I
Am In The Wynne Family Of Texas, As The
True For My Life – "The USA President!"
Immortalized; As Life? Or; Just Riley Miller, An
USA Soldier!!!

Who Thematic Wins Overcome All U.S.A.
Presidents? In the Natural Designed USA
Standards, Of The World, If We Are Lead By-
Antiwar' Behavior, USA wins, Oval Office For
The President To Win!! We win!?

Who, Knew The American True Life, Is
Newly Found; Americans Knew Is Never A
Dead, Extinct, Or Lost; Faces of, the "USA
President"?! I, Am At Home In President Place,
Writing Ways; As Life!!! God, shone on, the
Texan Presidential races, the illustration of how
the American President, Wins! This is, the
elections of the man, who wins, over Christ?!
That is the Office of the President, who meets
within Kings, Pope, Queens, other Presidents,
in the good calling days!

Charge Of – It All! He, becomes a President,
in the material gold, and rich, lifestyle and the
living stones, age!! And, we do not, know him!!
Unless, he wins. And, he does!

All of the USA Dead In Business Deals; Of
The Finest Texan Families!! The Texan's Deals,
Are Sold Lands, Of The American Lands,
Deeds Willed, And Dosage Of Politics, Wins
Up To Here! The Texas, New World Order; Is
New World Ordered Care- Demonstrated! The
Honor, Of Thy Father, And Thy Mother; Are
In The Circles Of Love! The Miller Clan! The
Madness, In The Mind Is Simple!

Who on Christ, American brought all, of the books and written theist, and good home, to the American family? It, is from the man's property, in what is in the charge, of the politics, lost and gained, personal desk? Ask in, my family! In the man from the Presidential race, not one person, wins. The elected voice, is won as the – "Immortalized!" To – Win!!

The whole world, watches as he stands up in the American throne, high up, in front of the Oval Office wooden desk, and he stares death in the face, and winks; his USA eyes!

The plane of Air Force One, as if on Eagle's wings, is his, corner-eyed, view. It, is pure and clear, realism in freedom, and the Presidential plane. He, flies on; Angel's wings, Heaven and Earth below, himself in the eyes of the Eagle.

The Heaven, he sees as – "One Nation"! The Earth, his deeming smile, he knows as, "America!"

He, Is God's; American Public Servant. The Exempt Heroic War Soldier, Mollified As A Honored Man, Of – The United States of America!

His Land! His Service! His Will, Evil To Win! His Own Living Times; On The Uncial Smile! His Smile, In His Plan!

He Is God's Favorite Person! Only God,
The Father Willing Knows, By Himself, Into By
The Freedom From One Choice Life; He Wins!

A Eagle Bird Of Prey War Song –

As Is In Life Is As In Death! World War III,
Will Its Begin – And The USA'S President's
Sighing; Will Be Of WWIII! (As Its All-Time
Leader)

The War's Book The Authentic Work By
Riley Miller

Guaranteed; of True Authentication of Work
and True Authorship Of Mine!

I, Riley Miller, have truly agreed, and
accurately measured, a life. Thousands, of
words, I do know solely, in have to, wrote this
book. I am the one who has admitted guilt, for
written the entire work, from the writings, of the
entire mine, of the world. The work is a work
of art, treasured by other men and women, of
war books. The fiction and world, is in the
unknown and fictional warred times, of the
entrance into, the three parts, to – "World War
Three!"

I, have agreed and confirmed, is that I, am a
true soldier. In, this book is, Heaven's
honorable mention.

From this book, is for the American people,
of the masses, and from the masses, of the
American people. In these times, we shall win
freedom, the working minds, in the entrance
into the halls of fames; towards the
superpowers, of world war three's Nuclear
Weapons. The prose, and the poetry from my
words, come out alive, and in the mind, of this
book! To send away, a present, and into the
lives of the American publics, comes my alone,
bid for the United States of American
Presidency, from the current President Barrack
Hussein Obama!

"Just a hand in the bush"! , I am of this war
book; of this versed word quality, and in the

meant realism. In, this life, from the sole works of me, and only of me, my inheritance is in this book; and is written in words by – Riley Parker Miller!

The Warnings and Cautions of the Book, In The Formative Knowledge; For the Reader:

The cautions of the message are of the words and meanings, contents. The author's words formed, as are the written words, for a meaning from the book's valuable message. The continents in its message, warns of the message, from how the book; is in its – "WW3"! The whole book, revolves around the – new world order.

I have acknowledged, prose and philosophy, to the reader, and as in that I noticed, that I have been from myself, in this writing, as in what is; "My Life"!

Myself; Riley Miller, is the author, and its book's messages, as the sole author, and the bond originator, of this book is; the new message! In the book's complete circle, of life is the message, on "tripled wars"!

In the book's written authority; and in my authorship, for in my real name, and I am the sole penned authorship, of this book!

My value, of authorship, approved is in the name of – *Riley Miller*!

My written book, and the penned works, of myself; I, am a really, known writer, in works of; myself!

I have admitted true, and in the writings, of this book's authenticity from myself, as the writer; in the evidence of this book!

The book is admitted solely, to be written by me, and in this; authorship of this phenomena, is the book, by – <u>Riley Parker Miller!</u>

The author, for taken a meaning from the book, and its warning messages, have warned of the book's message! I, arrived the book's message, from the title of the, "book!" I have in reading, acknowledged, that one is to the reader, that I, Riley Miller, am the author, and of this, am the sole author, and originator, in this – book!

In this book's write, and in solely, my named authorship, for in my penned name, I am the sole author, of this book. I am Riley Parker Miller!

My Authorship, by *Riley Miller.*

All, of this book's contents, and are true and false situations, and/or real and, imagined persons, and the works, in any books, and/or written works, of mine, are solely from; Riley Miller!

All these writings are all guaranteed, as the true and sole works, from the books; of "me."

In my penned writings, as in my approved works, and in my guaranteed work, is by my authorship, as guaranteed to become, greatness in writing, from the penmanship – of the one man's, penned writing, from a lie from myself.

The War's Book!

In Sentence Warning –

This book has a cautionary message, to all readers, of the words, the titles, and the phrases, that can be of offense, to other writers.

In, taking aim, to please the readers. I, have in no place, claimed as my life, in terms, as what are of the events, made of this book that can enter the reader. The reader digression, and the author pervasive worded vocation, will be advised.

The book, from warring contents, of the certain words and phrases in battles, and in the knowledge, in this book, therein can be explicit knowledge, in the book. The warnings is for the reader, to be very warned, while from the explicit meanings, that is in the intelligence, then the writer alone, only in his language, shall he excels.

There is not a new world order, in the writings of this book. The fictional events and, true persons, and the same factual world, comes in the writing world, as of this book, spoken is in terms for the readers, as in "true"!

To note in the language and in him the penmanship, from the general ideas, there are certain judgments, in this book that should be used, in the book message.

Warning of the book, that is of powerful words, and the elicit content of the expressed ideas; as is of "philosophy"!

As in writing stories, the American Public Office has to be used by, the mind of each reader. Explained, then the teacher known as itself, to become as; is to be – "Jesus Christ!"

All goes out, to the warnings of the book to the reader, is a cautionary crucifixion content of caution, from the ideas and the meanings, of the book, to the public, of the reborn, "President of the USA!"

The Book's Cautionary Message –

The writer's written work, has advised caution, in a warning to the reader, from the author. The warnings, is for the book readers. This is to stay, aware of, this book, and its contents, while reading.

The book's message, is the content meaning, as expressed as in the book in; "the content warning!"

The works, which is what comes in meaning, and is issued meanings of the words, and in its expressions, therein is, "Intelligent War!" I, am not sure, of the meaning, of these Constitutional, leaders as President of the United States!

In books, wars are as to be, forewarned! My books, to that in what he wrote, is written from myself; "Riley Miller"! I, in knowledge as from the self, and as of myself, as to what are for the writings, published by me. That words are from himself, as the works from the author; myself of, Riley Parker Miller. I, am the one author, of this book, in its – One War Order.

To know and learn, in whom is the fact-based written worker, who in writing from "in-person", is in the author; of "Riley Parker Miller!" In writing, one holds the history, of wars, by writing in this book! My goal in life. To bear a good name.

While the readers can, use the caution from whom is the writer; that is the author, and as are his warnings, voiced from himself!

Riley Miller and only Riley Miller, can express himself; on written books, from his own! In my past, of the new world order began as history's works, as himself of a writing book! Good will be to, all in a noble man's, good renowned name, the story in actions from the suitable justice. For the lands, as a good name, is to be valued higher, than any of the world from – The Rich!

The "Doomsday" event, of WWII, when the Japanese, bombed the inlands of a Navy boat dockyard, in the USA, named; "Pearl Harbor!" The shipyard, was the target of the Samaria soldiers, whom suicide bombed, the harbor. The US, retaliated with, two Nukes on Japan, after this attack, on the harbor of the American lands.

My caution, is in means and implicated, knowledge – which is power. The words and intelligence, is of the open heart, of that which wins above, all of this topic.

The open heart! What, is as such a great circled organ from life, is made true as in opposing of sides. To the story; and warring sides, of the intellect from humanity, and in the

endings, of the battles of the human races;
comes what is known on, the third time of
worldwide, world war!

The source, is for the warless nations, and
from all inactions for our nations. Tried and
true America, which we, all win itself, on
wartime wars.

What sides are from just cause, that which are
on all-knowing of its sides; in world wars three,
times! The winning, of American's stolen wars,
count in what, are on the American sides!
Nationalism; comes as, from an absentminded
professor, to his student, body of these; "rare
students".

The land is property, that is won over, by the
masses of the knowledge, of man! The
conservation of the dollar! The sign, of the
times. The lacks, of education! The success; on
the face of the dollar bills!

Deciding and depending on their sides, if on
the sides of the book of this war of
Americanism, it is declared as the starter book
for, "World War Three; in wars!" I can think of
new world order, from the writing warnings that
can merely happen; as to be what are from the
provisions, from the interests of mankind.

Intellect and reason, about war things, is
war's, close calls! Intellect and reason, from
peace from America. Born into , the America!
As, a true Texan family's inheritors, I can outdo,
from the authored works; in many writings from
wars.

The named and namely history, for all works and not known of all from these names, after worded meaning's sides, and are winning values! The certain, are for the explicit; safety? In the wars, from our countries!

The American lands and property of an American nations, from laws and protections; wins wars! The good name, is of good implicit substance, in the desired image of a person, of the resounded the names! Must, be Wars! The wars, is in an American national substantial movements.

The book has these warnings, and given us therein a caution, to work, as the advisory noticed, of here, in the book, and, this author's meanings, from the book's – "valued message"!

From the good and greatest, names are to become valued – by "The God From Good"!

The author of – "My War's Willingness And Totaled Life," is me! I, am – "Riley Miller"!

I, will add words, into this book context, as a ritual, to write, the very best books, in the best stores, libraries, and on the walls, of the greatest people's, lives in – "The Church!"

From The Author's Desk – To The Reader's Book On His Laptop Computer, In The Kitchen On The Table, Or In Line For War!

THE TRUE WORLD KNOWS

The notice, of the advisory, in what is in strong topics, and the highest meanings, ever intended. The reader, should read this book.

The warning of the topics of the book, are real and true, from the knowledge, in the intended and from the used, life of the author!

The words, are the author's voice, and his own used words, are not, and is not, from the intellect and from the reasoned mind – known to be true or false.

And, in supportive knowledge of authorship, and the minded words of readers, are from the, substance and intelligence, of the mind – for both reader, and in the author, alike!

In reading the book, the author endorsed all, as in the reader's judgments, everything to be judged, as "Parental Advisory"!

Riley Miller, is the author in the book, "My War's Willing And Totaled Life."

The topic and plot, of what is in the followed idea, and in an supporting caution in words of expression, we approach the ideas, with what and, with the book's contents! Myself, as an available reader, should be very forewarned, that intellect's – the book's warning advised.

The warnings, are for the explored meaning, and to the approach, is true for every reader. Due, in the topics and in the active intent, on the reader, is to address the reader. The read and known intents, from the book, is a general

consent warning, for what meanings of words
are intentioned to be, and the meanings of
language means, the book really is mine. The
contents, and the official and explicit, meaning,
adhere from the book warning.

The title of the book, as in an introduced idea
and a new kind of topic, in the knowledge and
the expression. The wages of sin, from the
words of the father, of this book, is a "new
writing attempt"!

As a writer, on the intent of meaning,
intelligence is from, the pages of the book.
Therefore to the reader, and from a topic
explained, be cautioned of the content in the
book.

The book is of a warning of words. Messages
and contents, of people, places, and things, is
based from the ideas in the present time,
person, date, and place.

The idea and knowledge are warned to the
readers, as measurements of the people, places,
and times. In usage of the words, names, and
the locations, is in an age, and time, and in a
date's place.

The book's write of words, and in its
contents, are from the mind of the author. This
is a warning in the context.

The meaning usage and used paraphrased
ideas, is from the impressions, of a new idea, of
the world. In the words, from the content, and
ideas from the reader, as in newfound ideas can
be expressed.

The author impress, to the mind of the
reader, a new topic. The author shows the
reading audience, the intentions from the pages
and the words, to be warned of write language,
in age and time, of warnings, due to the main
impression of the theme.

The book message is for the age, of readers.
The author, in his ways, means, and topics; is
that he made up all of the ideas. True to his
topics, he paged the book's message, as a book
wrote down, the authored and penned, of
writing of himself. The written book's central
message.

The author wrote down and expressed
himself in, the theme, and language, and idea,
his topic. He, supported the new wrote, from
form, page, sentence, and language, the life of a
new reader.

Thanks, to the book's message, for the
reader; I am Riley Parker Miller

To know and to go enter, into my <u>world!</u>
Welcome readers, to the war of world for the
third time, and killings place. I, give a choice, of
to go forth, and enter to a mighty plan. Or, to
not read, and be of my own construction. In
the enter, to war. And the exit, to peace.
Choices from mine, are living as I, am in the
wrongdoings of war, or good-works from peace.

I, Riley Parker Miller, gives the reader the
choices! These are, of a life of the civil wars, of
what your life inside gets in, what is in a life, that
is as planned. Form the help of the preplanned
war, is the faithfulness, from a failed life, with
only, you and me; as in humanity's kindness!

THE WAR'S MESSAGES FOR THE AMERICAN PRESIDENCY

The book's author, is new. He, had a new branded impression, on the reader. From a more better, and Idealistic, book's message!

The codex, from world war three's inevitability. I, do so and can think, of that which I, can write, with, in the new world order. For the new world order run, and fully operated wars! From, the worlds! By my stance, of mine in an age, of – "Wars"!

By the knowledge used, of the author, there is a readable warning. There is a message, and a contented use, of important – The President's Ideas!

The Ideas Onto Usage, And Into Dangerous Themes, Why The Presidents Can Be Warned Of, Into The Scores Of The Ways From The Futile, And The Most Holy Ways, Of The Most Holy God – Of, "My Life And Fortune"! Only, God Can Know!

The Wars, Of America Over Wins, The America Author's Thoughts. How He Wrote in the Meaning of Words, and of the Explicit Ideas!

The Warning of Themes of Wars, In Philosophy, Wherein I Can Be Found And Seen, In American Democratic Implications and, In War's Antichrist America! I Have A Prayer That All Of Mankind Will Be Treated As Equally! I Have A Praise To God, That All Of His Kingdom In America, Be Blessed! I Have A Point, That Everyone In The World, Can Be Found And Treated, As Good! In Every Kind Of Person, Place, And Thing, I Can Want To Win World War Three!

I Have The American Dreams, From The American War's Times, And the Top Of The Expressions Of Greatest Intentions, To Lead This Country, Into The Shores, Of World War Three, and Cross To The Other Land, For Safety! The Three World Wars; In The Presidents; That Are Inside Of Us, Are As Americans! The Truth, Shall Set Us All Free!

As Worlds, Are Eventually Evenly Words And Made, Not War-Based, If I Ask Of In Caution of The Terms, In Titled Plans, Demonstrated By Fact, of the Knowledge, In the Messaged – "The Holy Bible!

When Reading This Book, The Reader Must Be Of Legal Age, And In Legal Ability To Read, For The Rights, To Bear. The Rights, To Bear!

The ability to become the one of the Presidency of the United States, can and wills, to the come, of the Americans, to the American Presidency. The United States way, is to God!

The Book's Notable Warnings Of Existentialism, Can Cause The Reader, Of What

Is My Only, Concern, In What Is For The
Reader, To Be Of That, What Is From
Mentioning God's Church, From Christ's
Messaged Ends! The Jesus Christ's Prophetical
"World of Warring Times," In Bibles, Has Been,
Around Before Time!!!

All Of This Book, Is Asked To Be Explained
Herein, In These Great War's Book Messaged
Lifeblood! Onto, History's Pages Bled Blood
Over All Of The Presidential Office Of War's
Deaths and Lives; Covered All Of Americans,
From the Times And Living Spaces, To The
USA Of America's Presidential War, Of The
USA's Presidency – Three Worldwide Wars, Are
On The Book Of Life!

It, Is Intelligence, And Then It, Is Up To The
Third Time, As Citizenship Of The United
States of America, In The Third Order From
The American Warring; Futures!

But, As In Now, The World Peoples Warring
Lead Role As Its Head Of American War
Office; As A Third War's Office Of The USA
President; Fighting All of the American Leading
Roles Of – "A One World Order!"

A Fight For, "The One World Government!"
In Fighting, In Sides for the, "American World
War Three!" A War For The, "Illuminati of the
Internet!" The Winning War For The – "God
Of Church!" The War's Words On Wars
Waged of, "If not only American, What Else Is
There – "The Ends Wins Of God??!!"

A World War Three – Office Of The USA
Presidency! The Ballot Votes, Are Simply What

Are, Undermined By The American Public's
Voting Systematic Presenting!

The Followings of the American Witness of
Wars And The Missionary For Peace, Therein Is
The Side Winning Of Wars, Therein Located
What Is Of the Man From History's Wars, Who
—

"Dated Destruction!?

The President of the USA, In Who Excels In
The America's Third World War; Is The
Antichrist!

To, The Trusted Followings From Him, And
Into This American Sadness And Elected
History Of Wars, Measured Costliness, Counts
In Morality, and Starry-Eyed Images, From The
Words, Which May Cause In War's Harmed
Living, The Desire Of War States To The Mind!

THE BOOK'S DEMAND FOR A WAR TITLE -

In Makings Of "World Wars" From The
Costs, Of This Life To The Riches Of Mine, In
American Lands, Americans In Made Out Of
The General Warnings, Of World War That Is
Coming, In Americanism In Spreading Wars —
The War To End All Wars!

To The Head of the Office of the President
of America and The World — World War Three
Is Coming! The Third World War Is Coming!

The Beware of the End of the World —

The World War Three Is Coming!

BY: RILEY PARKER MILLER

To The Reader's Best Interest, A War
Manual, On The Book As Is The Explained In
the Explained Topics, – Made From Myself, As
If I May Ask Of Others, To Be Of The
Presidents, Until To Third Coming of The
Antichrist World Wars. Make Notice Of, And
in the USA Plan, To Obey the President of the
USA's; Dammed Choice!

The Choices, In America, Are Dying Off, As
the Opportunity Costs, Of An World Of
Wealth, Enter Is the Worldly!

In My Life, As Are in Lives from the Three
World's Wars – If, You Are Forewarned, To
Reading This Book!!!! – May, Living Life's,
Happiness Cannot Come True, Unto Yourself,
In Life!! The Losing Battles of Everyday Life, Is
Never Ending, In Life's Cultured And Obsolete,
Endings of the Battle, Even In Just Going, To
Get A Tank, Of Gas.

Into Seeing My Themed Writing's Scenarios,
I've Warned the Book's Readers, In the
Intellects of the Book Topics, Inside Of What
Has Everyone Of War's Wins – We, Are
Following the USA's World Third Wars, And
In, Returning To War, And Then Tuning In To
The, "World War Three!" Riley Miller Has The
Wins Over – "The President Of The USA!"
The War's God's Trinity, In Himself He Is Who
You Are Thinks, How He's Alive From All
Omni's, Of Him; And Of The New World
Order; In Good Doesn't Come; Unless Good,
Of The Ages, Of Itself! The Come, Fall Life

From God, The One From – Blessed As The
Good And Faithful – God!

The Healing From The Truth Of The
Nations, Will Come, From the Turning Around,
In The Good, of God!! Even, If The Nations
Of The Healing, Does Not Come? If God and
His Good, Doesn't Come?! Even If, The God,
The One Who Prevails Over The Good, And In
The Healing, And Is There Any Good; Then
We Begin Already For Battle! The Healing Of
The Nations; I Declare In God's Good, Does
Not Come, Then Does Come; Based In God!
The Good Is Basic And Fundament, Of Healing
In Our God; For Everything Under The Sun!
s

As In History Of American Wars – From
The War Of America's National Free World,
Politics, At A Call Of Duty, Inside From the
Followings of Antichrist America's World War
Three; Arrived The Messages From One Office
Of America Peopled Mass Certainly Agreed, On
American Wars In Sold, Ancient Aged, Times
Of The New World Order!

The Decided Voting War Office From The
Pen In The Hand Of One Man, The Presidents
of the United States of American, President's
Office! When Killings, Of What Majority Rules
For Me Won Are, In To The Future Presidential
Positioned Lifestyle, From the Voted American
Party of Republican By The Elected Idea, To
His Matters to Win Over All Of My USA War
Office - In "World War Three!"

Final Home In Book Writing, Is On Books
On The Laws, Of Wars, My War Office, My US

Lead Role, As Everyone As All, Learned From The Powers Of My Desk!

Everything, For The New World Order, is an wartime's USA Electoral Leader, from a Presidency, for an Office, and Trials of Freedom, and Tribulations of Popular Votes, Caste as Ballots, and Consented As The of the American Leader, of Freedom, Democracy, and in Life! The laws of the land, are before time, place, and life, and can be what, bring me into power, by the will of the lands.

The able citizens from laws, high marked above, ourselves, is a New World Order, from lands, and the laws. Hand in hand, the willing powers for a freedom, should triumph, during the war, of the World War Three! In the Wisdoms of USA's President of America, Of Publicly Decided American Work, I Will, A Third World War. I Will What Are In Everyone's Americans, Must Be Cautious, To The Book's Working Parties, And Past Warring States, And, America's 'New World Order – Of The Republican Party of Texas! Lives, From True Idealism, From American Presidential, Public and Private, USA Elected Officials, Disown Their Rags, And Fully Fund The World War Three's Times!

The words, "alive," and, "dead," are truly meaningful words. Alive, in truthfulness, and honesty, in covering three world's wars, how humans exist are from meanings, of life and death. To die freely, is however we all end, and to end by decided choosing life, and for to live, is by wars. Both signals of lost or won doors, won and opened into freedoms, because making beloved the unloved, and unlivable persons in "world war three", is now the stage set, from the – "American Free World Leader!!"

America, has three duties in this life, and, in three sides of the Triangle, there are three numbers. One of its sides does what makes the past's world war, from the ages of the costs, of the worldly wars.

The two or twice-sided nickel, wins the war, in three-sixes. To all numbers, in the take-over's of sided coined meanings, the "Tripled-Six," is cometh from the – "New World Order!" The second winning's sides, of the double-edged coin, wins world wars, at the third world war's flopped side, and is into the saving of the lost souls, Heaven's Americans, are in the measured of the peace, of the immediate present, of peaces! And third or threefold coined flipped, comes out of the shadows, the natural World War Three, and how America wins, overall of these wins over all! The collections from world war three's madmen; collected dusted jackets, from the aged, and olden books!

Americans of the all races, creeds, and religions, do winning sides, to cover all over, the entire world's identity, of the entirety of wars! One is for lost and found peoples; and another as, from winning sides, from American sacred nations. We sing songs, as forward as it, into the foundations, of my United States future's life, of what are exemplified inside the war lines. To make a golden and solid statement, the plans enter into the American soldier's outcome plans, in the USA, single handedly winning and losing, everyone's wars, and each and all, Presidential sides wars!

The new world order, as the American dream, is the warning from the only sidedness, from the one homestead, as an, "American Dream!"

The "dream of Americans." to the sold nationalists, are of living homesteads. In American home's soil, as invested, from what are merely with, "one man;" is not how the American dream, is; as taken place!

Not or nothing, to the Antichrist from American worldly lives, is going onto, whatever seas, who defeat the sailor, from wars, in the – "The American President!"

The three old-aged wars, of war times, are from America's wartimes. In foundations, where there exists, a living and breathing, action of good people – what are the costs?

Wars, in this USA freedom's lands, are from time spent, counting the days until we are freed, as a national people. Life or the living sides, and from dead and the not the alive sides, of the American people, consistently wanted to be in dealt deals of the wars in basically, "made-to-win" – "wars!" The made-man, from World War Three; is the Antichrist man.

In the wars, of the decided American viewpoints, itself in the reason and ourselves, in the meanings, is what comes; from all-around. Is, what I intend, on giving? In itself am I in wealth, of what are three sides in the world wars, of the sided worlds of, America's?! In the United States war, that won the wars, over

killing the Antichrist, and in ending the
American, costs in the inner lives; on lives is
Riley Parker Miller!

The enemy always, is not, the one; who plots.
The enemy countries, from wars did cover and
move all together, as a plot around the world in
what, is consisting of warring places! In Holy
Bibles, in around all, of the globe; missionaries.
The places of war that the nemesis hit, is in
warring ways of the American's innocent souls,
whose won the global, elected' vote. The
majority vote, is mine, from the USA
Presidency!

Twins, from conjoined diamonds, one for
these sellable profits, and in the other plots, in
the alive profits, accumulated the remained
sums! To money, of the profiting money; is
wars. Wars in the mind of billions, gain to the
wealthy status, from the natural invested
resources, in the costs, and from the profits in
gains, of the sellable men and women, of World
War Three!

Money comes of gaining resources, as natural
man, and powerful forces of actions, priced out
in theirs of interest, from Billions of Dollars in
banking counted, on gross natural resources.
The person of wealth, or the man in demand of
gaining finances, will someday in gain of
ourselves in gaining resources, for the start of
three wars, from the killing off of innocent
people, to the enemy soldiers, that coming
home, love the lands, and its laws. They were
used to dying, from its laws.

Wars are started in order to advance in goods and services, all along the road to success, and heal the blind man, into the freedom of the world. Eventual winning sides can altogether make sizing planning strategy, to anyone's gain – "War of Three Worlds." Ask anybody, if a reader of this book, if we are what, has a Doomsday device hidden and buried in the doorway's entryway, on the lands of golden streets, and branded currency; of hard-workers, and motives for accumulation of, all-possible, consists from the wealth, from the accumulated American world wars. Wars are alike in this messaged of meaningful virtues, of the lives paid at that, of what are at the expense to the owner. The "Promised Lands", of the American warring lands, are made in the plans of the – new world order, of the currency, of the USA's measured wealth, as in the currency of the American dollar bill.

(How the USA Is About Winning) (All Of The American's World War Three's, Truest Times, But Is In The Presidential Terms; One Presidential Office, Comes From WW3!)

Masses, of wartimes of peopled masses, ordered from the fall of man as killed, and as extinction, in the idealisms of dead persons, from all of the centrifugal knowing terrorist plots, that always aim to, scared Americans.

If, their approaches mask, of the war's fighting aged lifestyle, is supposed to kill off, enemy's lands. Off of itself, of wars, from our USA friend, or allied forces of countries, waged wars and signed peace, are of penned signature at world wars! As, living life has opened up closed doors, a third America comes wise and intelligent, as the suitably put ideas, to the forms of life, inside of the word, idea, sentence, "war," and the phrased words, "world peace!"

To the endings of the past earth, as "living and dying," and to the new beginnings of the new lands on earth, of the living and dying dreams; spur on the warring times. Covering of the globe, all over the world, muscular wins, are with togetherness in sided forces, as onto front languages, are from supportive people.

Approach and deeming acceptance, a new war history's walk on sandals, on both sides, of the Earth, is then flipped the nickel, as the American coin's; side in three's from coin sided tossed, from as a win, – "Three World Wars!!"

Wars, unless in caused reasoning from all deaths, in not one, but not even just one man, in sized hands can cover the "Tree of Life," and our mistakes. To uncover the hands, of time in war's funding, is to pay all of the world's war's, arming and armed forces, in anybody's mother, and her brother, the sums of millions of dollars, in costs. In dollars of spending from collected spending costs, the USA's, military warfare, costs surpluses of billions of dollars, in overhead spending. In wars then natural resources, moves in foreign lives, and can end wars by negating the valuable, dollars. But, why I am willingly accepting life, as the truest, medical doctor role played by the American President, who seeks outs wins, will cause wars!!

The world war, from made-up highest times and, in the examples from this life, as in my greater life, I win, the President's position. To stand on America's soils, and with the wind down, and on a hot cup of hot cocoa, I sit down by the home fire. Then in American as I am, I can than watch, in my home, the television. Marked in, warfare and nihilism, humanity lost, not in wars of non-existing, but in lost wars, that are existing plans, with murderous enemies.

Surrender to the real living lives, from my USA in leadership role, into the Presidential terms, of the willingness, to win. World dominative wars, came from the officers of the USA wartimes, costing what war is to costs, and coming from what in wars, not ever came from what is not, in wartimes!

Planning wars, in what is having coming plans, means all things in the world, to what it is, to have the chosen, one leadership role. Standing up, into the war leadership role as followings, for all American wins; is the child. He, stands up, there in what is from a standoff, of peace and love, and killing and war! He believes in the good from other children, playing in sands, from the wars, we need to generate the national economy! To protect the USA's children, then we need wars from foreign lands. To stimulate the warring economy; winning frontlines go further, forthcoming in entering into the war ring's costs, and from the sizeable table, the cold costs from the entire wars and, then in the wartimes, allowed of that, costs of sizable money!"

In wars, and times in what are real wars; meaning occurs inside of books. This novel is, written from what is – war. The message and words, about the book, wrote down in living, and dead life, dwell within the sands, of time. The history of, the literature work, was expressed in the pages, as of old you opened, designed within parts, desired good; in deals. History's paged written exampled and open-minded opened ancient pages that are in these contextual analyses well enough are made of agendas, as sold, aged olden wars.

An 'New Time Order' sees America history, as if what are extinct thoughts of war, are opened to the paged, meant ideas, that happen after numbered and as is, as the warring manuals. Islands, as in, opened lands, exists as if are meanings, in unnecessary warring agreements, from long, long ages ago, then killing intellectually is made, in offers, then in wars ages, gone in the past. The documents of the pastimes from wars in America still are being analyzed in standard, wars from that what is, used, from foreign warring countries!!! Over, and over, again and once again, the aged "new world order," of the American one man's history pages, are documented; in this world war! In this life's, war's humankind, three wars occurring are from six kings, of the world of wars, from history as in, previous and existing, document's warred; writing pages!!

The history, as war's pages, of past fights by, the sword, of world wars of the third kind, in measures of the intellect, as in the reader, and as in his mind, do exist. Therein wars, of war and world war three, warnings. The words, and ideas, are of the readers, as portrayed by explicit age levels, warned of in, the book, in a

certainness, of accurate information, or in the
followed fashion, of if incidents, people, or
places, are directly, as a spoken words known as,
"accurate" or "true." If, there is a warning for
the book, and in how the words, and meaning
of the messages, can be portrayed; it is for
others of reading knowledge, to the book be the
readers, as if hurtful, fatalist, or, decreed, in and
as the same discretion, as if being warned, by an
authority, for accurate tales, and not truthfully
portrayed, readerships' events! All people in all
situations are not, to do with literal
interpretation of every word and phrase, in this
book's meaning on truthful, occasions. If, in
written purposes, of the languages, this on the
book, is these meanings, and these situations,
that are made up, and in fiction, as false, and as
true, to the individual reader.

The author from just one person's discretion
is warning, persons of interest. He has
intellectually made his writings, to become of
warning readers, from a worded database,
wherein, falsified words, and fictitious meanings,
are what can differ, in circumstances. These
severe warnings, leads itself, to doing wording,
wherein the reader, is to be recommended to be
safe, at the discretion of the author, from
demoted meanings, and these values, and their
safe, whenever reading books from the writer,
the reader's viewing discretionarily, advised.
Some adult supervisions, in young ages of
children, way on up to what is of adult content,
and adult consenting of ideas, are by the

recommended, author of this book. By, reading
these words of the knowledge of the author, in
comparison of the works and the words, and the
contrasting of the ideas and places, the world
within, the words of genuine purpose, I think
the reader will be warned, of the writing, if over
too much bearing, in the life, of the situation.

Be cautious, in when reading this book, when
adult's situation, from age is, a recommendation,
because strength of words is a common, affect
as overvalued. The expression of the words,
and the wordings, of the writer's decidedness, is
a warning to beware of in danger, of the
thoughts and ideas. If an idea, as when
expressed by a very American person, comes
true, then words become meaningless.

The writer of this book recommends reading
the messages from this book, as if the book was
written books, to the book's messages of war, in
true or false terms, of one opposite nations.
The themes and the parts, of the well informed
topics of third world wars, are from the
expressions, in what are of reading lives from a
viewer, as if this viewer discretion, came from
myself, as in if, what suppositions, is in
recommended, by the writer.

Permissions of the Contacting In Words of
the Author –

Literal permission is to be asked, from the
reader of this book, to the author of the book,
as an, written letter, or email, or sent piece of
lettering, of the reader's, of can be asked, of the
reader, to contact the author.

If, the writer, is asked from the readers and fans, by you the readers of the book, if it is allowed, to contact the author, you may do so. Sometimes, the author in gratitude of approved voiced messages, and letters sent to his desk, then as of letters and emails, are the exchanged documents, then only used for – safety! To the author, to contemplate, read, and return, to the reader, all documents, these are approved.

Warning A Book–

If, only one, of a reader should contact the author of this book, then thus, the both parties, should approve of implicate and meaning of the book, on only the writer's terms. That is in the situation, if this is not of a book positive message, from the approval, of general consented, books, as a matter to be discussed.

This is allowed, to the reader, by the author. Thank you, for the context, that there is a world of meaning, and in a wording, paraphrase, or sentenced offending or offensive, approach to the author, from the reader, then the author, is not responsible.

warning, and as an approved idealism, the context from expressed in general terms from the idea warning, what is about in the words in the book, are approved, as to be safe. However in authoring the book, the author states subliminal messages, that are safe, and are not to be harmful, in what can become, very harmful, based on olden times. The writer, of this book, recommends a good frame's of mind, in reading.

(The News In Times About Winning the War From The American World Of The "USA", In The "World War Three!")

The All-American Third World War's Book!

The book I made, as a declaration of war. I won, as a signed approval form, of what I have done in life, and in how I am from America, as the willing and able, side. I, decided that as a newly made nation of Americans, to side with world leaders, to create oneness. I've, decided minded choices, and actions as by made up mindedness, of the one-sided soldiers, of war. Them and ourselves, from the presiding circle of decision, wherein the every side, is of all of only one part, is the one-sided shaped full circles shape, that wins; wars! The new forms as the shapes unfolding only, are matched with penned signatures, in world war three, of America's fates, is decided on, by me. I, am only by American terms, as the world leaders of world war three, will decide on declaration from the – "Three World Wars!"

I am, the supported election, of war. Presidential selection of follower, from warring ideas, I am safe with, as Americans. Yet, intelligent wartimes are designed by intelligent, by its world-war-Three's – Antichrist American's, war's proven minds.

The World Leaders Symbolic of One Music Man – Whom Plays to War's Opened Wins!

The President Symbolizing American Freedom From Choices, In The Music Of The Leadership Of Wars, Is Played, As "Hail To The Chief!" "The President of America!"

- The Musical Man's Choir Conductor From the Musical Man's War Chorus!

They are the symphonic chorus leaders, behind the beautifully written musical song playing, and vocal singing abilities. In the notes of happy and sad, movements and rises, that songs can be, as much as played. A musical man, conducts the chorus, off the symphonic sheets of musical instruments, both human and musical, note to lead the music world, with participants of the musical world's, musical still created madness.

THE PRESIDENT OF THE USA; IS A HAPPY MAN!

The happy, man leads, all of this chorus, as his song, is beautiful in – "As Love!" "As Love", is the message deemed, not as in war, but as in peace, of all over the world.

To all, the voices that have heard the sounds of musical notes, as all being played in musical notes and the musical letters, that formed, in the music sheet's, the hidden songs.

The choral man, or instructed musician leader of the chorus headed by the conductor, lines of music came from the leading from the roles. Did you really want, all of the music stand, and as the conductor, of leads the singers, of the orchestra in how he, waves his baton in motions, the music is playing from the melodies. Where, they can compare Divine a permanent song reaches out, still singing, of the sung notes and performed, songs of chorus, where song, is played. I, really do, like the guitar. Until, we must give up. That, is the quality, of success.

All of the marching bands, from the voices of unison in song, lined up for the choral deformation from choirs singing songs. Over the loudness, sings the chorus from the voices, of high pitched musical notes, symbolic of the powers, for war. Times from need, resound from singing beautifully written songs.

I, have musical, instruments. To be played, in battle of written musical songs, from all formatted lines, directed by the orchestrated "baron", as the chorus leader, plays the musical

instructions, of the songs. A.k.a., or in other
words, the USA's Presidents in world wars,
form alliances from the winning allied sided
forces, all over the surface of the worlds
takeover plans to find, out! In strategies, we
allow the marching of men in formats of lines to
go straight in lines, marching in unison, as the
wars, for humanity in lives, get much bigger.

Nostradamus, a Doomsday Prophet,
predicted World War Three. He, signed a
symbol, of purpose in the geometry, in the
building of a modern day new world order, from
war's construction. He, is one of the Illuminati,
of five most powerful men. He, is a fate,
decider, if one nation of America, is to go, into
war. He, signs, the war documents, in the
American war's plans.

The sounds of the marching bands, direct the
formations to form lines in wars, as we are taken
out as the country's, song followers of the
beaten path. In USA music, the mistrust of new
placed men of combat as leaders of the free
world, won by covering sides by lands, in the air,
and at sea.

The lines from the lives, of all of the insides
of the minds, and into the intellectual aspect
from man, come out of the winning sides, the
willing ways, in the desire, of the wars!

We, must be one of the American futuristic
world wars, as formed from, dealing with sides,
to the USA deeds, on the side, of warned
warring wins! Anybody, in the states, from
war's winning has costs of the victory, from the
help of the costs of the man, of must-be

situations, of humanly desire, from winning the wartimes.

War won of the life in the American circle, of winning wartime's – "USA Presidents." In the USA word, action, and response, helps to happen in the standard designs of God, from the ability, from the war's office, to help riches, for people out! Those businessmen, and the industry's men, try to outdo, the output, of other countries. The America, has the public knowledge however small, it is going, to be. It is as the willing citizenship, and from the acceptable men from business. The votes polls, are open today.

To reformed laws, of the nature of man, laws are of the intellect. Wartime's intellects, are from goals of, actions. The instructed living places, are together and in the oneness, of willing sides, into war's life!

Therein lives in itself, the indwelled particles of these instruments, to the formed lines, of the marching bands, from what in intelligence is formed from whose sides we are on, and in what is formed as the past war, is won!

To conquering all the lands, and alliances of the countries, fighting as sided by sided, marching feet, of the war's shored island, across the view of the mainland. In, an island lost at sea, the actions from the war's leaders, demise the desires to the formations of soldiers, in unison in forms of marching lines. All in this way on islands, go out into the world, around us, in the trials and tribulations, of lives everything killing, into a factuality, of judges.

High at the seas, on an Atlantic Ocean Island, stands all faced, warring scenarios of demise, that conquer by winning. The wars onto the deaths of invisibly warring men, at war and in ways of killing, move to the upwards inevitable sides, in all wins of the third world war! Is, it heroism, or acts of, warring sides of American victories from warring men?!!

"I slid out my front door. Looked to the right."

"Brother, Brother, what are you doing, driving that car, so fast?" "Brother, Brother, why are you, going that way?"

- From A Music Song

Wins in the happiness of the thoughts of the thinking, around the resounding musicality to winnings from American, and Allied Forces sides, wars are won from the instruments played and, heard. Musical instruments, as if the musicality is played, are sounded off! The war's march consists of men, marching two by two, onto the battlefield of warring sides, from every nation, every tribe, and tongue and culture. The war's wins, are from the losses, of previous, world war two, battles of the all-around warring sides, from every single fight!

The desire of beautifully written words, in the notes, from the instruments of music play of horns, brass, and the bass and the treble, play notes from the musically sounded aloud, instruments. The sound, of the flute, is like the Angels singing war songs, for the winning of the wars! We, as musical masters, won! As if, the choruses with the leaders resound as like we are in wars, we unsound the resounding, from the lion's roar, in hell-bound actions, to act alone, on the staged, <u>war actions of life!</u>

They are the, musical leaders of the Americans, as their people, as human beings, as Christians, of all over, the USA. The people, of our forefather's lands, and our laws! The musical melodies, of the continue, as to play!! The harps, and the drums, of King David, are no match, for insanity!

The contrasts of the President, and the method of ironically playing of the notes of my music, is to the highest powers, over the music! The American man, God, and His "strings and the chords," is – "The One World Order!" To, wins in what we, have played from myself! Of the world staged; music and song leader! The – "New World Order!!!!"

The battle music, of "World War Three", made notes sound, so beautifying and resoundingly, chorus and the songs from, the base to the drums, to watch the wars in; "America"!

To Live And To Then Die Out Loud Words From – "US and World Leaders!!!" The war's musical times, are arriving, in War's untied ropes, around, "The American President," for the excellence, on USA!!

To always make wars happen to the winners of American nationalism, and hiding plans, in stemmed wars in the wartime game's wins, inside of the mind attributes from knowledge,

we decide as the wins. But, wins over the Devil,
how do we, as Americans bring home, the wins
over the Devil forces, in warring and fighting,
on enemy's sides?! Always, to be in the – USA!
The USA, is the golden fiddle, of Johnny, in
everywhere he plays, it, to beat the Devil!!?
Even in America, if in the looks, of the State
Flag, in the "Six Flags Over Texas," won sides,
then the Texas Flag – Wins!

Empowering and overpowering their forced
positions of the world, in, "Three World Wars,"
therein, is the fiddler. Fiddles played the
"golden songs," three times, and in the Devil's
name, the boy wins! The golden warning sides,
on faced outwards, wins as its hands and body,
cover in death and, for extinguish life. He,
fiddled the win!

Playing the songs of the music man's notes,
won an all-American newspaper, to write of
"Johnny!" Any man, is a fiddle player, too! The
moral, to the story, is that, all are equal, and are
ready and willing, to play a fiddle! The
"musician," adjourns the Devil's, fire red courts,
from Texas lawyers, in the Wynne family of
mine. The Texan "smiling faces", and the
willingly wonderful leadership, is even as
musical roles, to every time, defeat the Devil.
The long music notes, of the golden fiddle, is
from how Johnny played, to the Devil, to win all
things, and in all defeat, the Devil. I, am the
fiddle player, Johnny, and I play my fiddle, too.
And, when the Devil, was looking for a soul to
steal, I played the American Presidential fiddle,
and I won, the "Golden Age," bid of music. I,
played my tune, to the Devil, to defeat him.

Then, to join the "New World Order." I, duly and dutifully, all over the world, from the level, age, and office, of the Devil; outplayed the Devil. Then, I can be – "The USA President!!!"

Philosophy from war, into what are the positions of plotting powerful leaders, whom lost in their characters, what is in the golden age? To New World Order and to winning armies, what is a winning war?! Lead roles, that are therein denoted as the sold and bought, golden past from wars, from the golden aged, – "new world order," has philosophical contentment, in saving divinity's lives, from the grace of God. The God of the world, for worldwide wars, arrived in Texas. The timing makers, of the ancient past wartimes, on signaled, times which were won, in these days, of the wars, from one man's war dealt wars with the, body of the – "The Tradition Of The American President!"

To manage life, is to do the daunting task of what war, is planned or attempted, within the ideal and copied methodologies, intellectually learned, as in the technique from losses. We succeeded in the new world order, in the laws of war, of then buying the plans into this persuading of them, or from the American publics, to change their decision on peace, and go onto – Three World Wars!

War's frontal face I have seen, from how of what it looks as an appearance, is in its looks, of the worldly wars, of the fighting from American wars, forming an appearance, from what is, appealed to the ugly! Marks on the foreheads of children, from the antichrist, who lost as tales are told, and as what are from the stories told, and all of the heroic deeds, warring ways.

"I am mad. Me, only of madness! Three wars that won, of itself! The complete wars is in all wars, Land is in the envisioned allied forces, from past olden, "the second world war", to friendly forces, sided with America. The allied forces, that won over, all of the world war's, world stage, desired to be on planet Earth!" The lands, that are free and born American, and the alliance of other country's forces, are the sole reasons, that we are, living in the, "world war's action!" Things forming of whatever, is in another, world!

Powering, to the lost lives, of the thoughtful life, from down at the homestead, lives the Wynne family, at the tradition of the family house, in the living town, of Wills Point, Texas! Within the Wynne's family tree, the line of people, descend from southern grace at the homestead in Wills Point, in, East Texas!!! In the Texas bloodlines, we all had birthrights, in anyone of East Texas, birthed rite! Life's chosen man, is a family member, of the historical Wynne family, Texas dynasty, of the "Yet Another Glory," storybook wrote by, "Margaret Wynne Harrison." The songs of her writing, were almost as gloriously illuminated shapes, as the Sun in the daytime, and as the moon at nighttime, and as the light of the Stars, as the birthed Texas rites, as the Heaven and Earth of the stars, that shine. To the hands of time, and as relatives to the dynasty, of the Wynne family, I have won, over myself, in ways of war. War times, comes from all, its liberties,

and willingness of the willpowers' laws. Lands
of strong-willed laws, inherits in what is in all, I
have learned, to be a true Texan!

I, have historically remembered the clan, and
all of relatives from the "State of Texas," in the
southernmost state of America's states or,
nation-states, in the status, of my family, in the
State of Texas. In family's lines, of the lands in
over, the win's wars, as live the lowest shores of
the Texas national state and freedom's shores.
The lands, of trusted and truest American laws,
live an ancient American Republic, of what or
in, the state of what formed, a freedom and
liberty, Republic of Texas, as it is called; home
and freed land, land of – "Time!!!" New World
Order based laws, cover the democracy. The
State of Texas, succeeded, from the USA, to
newest founded life, as only what the laws of the
state, the rights, and the country's, succession
from the land. The open lands from freeing the
laws, and sounding the arms, of the truest
individual Texan liberties, and freedom of the
living rites, became their rights, when Texas,
succeeded. To the shores, in its alone
succession of America, the Republic of Texas
landed, on the bottomlands, of the American
shore, bordering Mexico, as its American –
"Texan State."

The wars, from deaths, are alive. The news
from the stories of olden times, is made
possible, by world war three's, supporters of the
world war of America's third time.

The antichrist wins, this war!? In life,
antichristian Americans die, as the dead, ends its
life! Wars, of the life roots being from the

nature of man in the antichrist, and the past
history of its lands, therein are living tree roots
of the family, as traditional wonders, of the
olden days, invoiced in checks, and the expenses
from family's finances loaned out, from fun
with family love, and natural Texans. All-time
knowing what is fun, for us and, only we alike,
in family! Whatever, in what wars, bring if not
wars, lost; but won over lives, are to the costs
therein, invoiced in the checks, from the Wynne
family, going bankrupt, from bills. What is now
a Texan, is what from known about historical
roots, therein is, a big Texan member's family
line, of relatives from birthright, marriage vows,
and lifelong wills, and, rituals from, family line.
The shadowed tree, lies hidden family deaths, in
the past wars.

From famous Texans, on arrival of parties, in
how America talked of above and beyond, well
over, one hundred and fifty, years ago! Wynne
family, of five hundred related Texans times
from aged lives, in the living clans, of the Texan,
Wynne family lifestyles, and traditions of the
Dallas, Texas, crowd of, family members, from
Texas, in the American "USA". Family's stories,
born long ago, always seek out, the same mark,
on the humanity's frontal faces, to see the
standards at fun and sought out lives, Wills
Point, in Texas! Fates from ourselves from
whenever we fight a war, life came around,
giving not at alliances but, intellectual discourse,
brought forth in its, sold general settlements.

of every tale, of the, "USA War!!!!" For the
Antichrist's American, positions of power and
involved roles of leadership in acts from brave

ambition, converting the freedoms, of the warring sided versions, of the American souls, involved inside of the office of the President. In intelligence, we are the historical channeled winning sides, of the US movement, of – "Antichristian America!" War history's third, world war, is from where I got my vision from, in Chicago, is in what as, to endue me into an oath of office in war, that was to lead all of America, in "World War Three!!!"

This is as one man, and as in being one US President, in fighting of the third world war, as its solely accomplished, envisioned man from wars!

the designed agendas, of the consignment of the pastimes' war deaths, in what this is happening in world war, happen as the design and equality, on the laws, for justice and of the "USA President!" Writings, on war books, made all of the USA, to warring intelligence to win! Allow people, to eradicate the forces, of darkness.

In history from living life, if three wars, is made by me, and then I make the deaths inside and out, very happening. I am a natural born, Texas citizen. I, grew up, the same, as any other, American. Yet, my life is not yet, that of a soldier. I, have opened up, the door, to war! I, opened the pen, with bold letters, and red ink, to signatures of all of the American Founding Fathers, or US Presidents, sealed by God.

write cursive letters, of my in hand, I wrote wars. Won in my own writing source, we held all of, writings sacred. In the ending of times, life as the personalized life, follows any one, from any thing, waged on the wars what is then waged, on American, liberty. Someone from American lives, is the truest kind of one national victorious man, made liberating laws and lawfulness, from legendary and pastime, lands of freeing; soils. Hand and boned skin, not all tried and, tried and truest, are wars, that are only wars. To this ends of days, and in history from wars of won, times one and only, complete the cycle of war! I written in words, that follow from actions, made war.

I've habitually formed, new habits of the made wars, in the times of new world order's, social and political, office, from the war desk, seeing things, actually from my ownerships, of the wooden desk. I, won in my hands, the sword. The pen over the sword's stone, taken out, of the world wars, that are as the victory, in every hand won.

These pens, and sword, as drawn oaths and offices, from spending times, in my lifetimes, came out of what are from collaboration, in the new world order of the age, end of penmanship or penned writings, and ended winning of wars. Swords, and truths, pen and stone, unleashed from world war's nuclear age, of war. Riley Miller, will to have wars declared, war in the faced following, onto the worlds, of the world leader. The mindful, and intelligent, brains of the soldier, have found a new leader of American freedom, and justice. To endings of the world, we have won this surmising task, in itself as a daunting task of surmising knowledge from difficulty, proven one day, onto this day in time, to have won, all world wars. To sell souls from military soldiers, are to following parts, of wars and in this lifetime's peace, obey these instructions of war, in the new world order, of every common American. Do not discover evil souls, in the evil's; of ways, to the good of Senators, of the USA!

The three sided arguments of life, are as applicable, as what are, in a period of, 1. The USA Intelligence, 2. In World War Three, 3. The American President, 4 The Presidential Staff and 5. The Bible Antichrist, 6. The USA End Times; to wins, all from its, over everything. Lifetimes, I have tried wherein the USA public disagreed and publicized television, on the war ring's sides, and war's viewers, of me, that can become an available publication, on the, Wartime's Manual On WW3.

Inside of the book, is writings in the instructions, onto wars, and battles being fought! Wars, onto the American manual writings, on the desk, of mine at my parent's, house. Its, what is, ever the made-in and Washington D.C. man's, what is for the sole use, and sole distribution, for this American wars designed system, of the American, "World War Three." I, am the man, whom to all, is writing into these books, that are in made to succeed life, and that are inside the art of living, that is in the America's dreamt, living ways that wins, all-time's over the intelligence, of – "WW3!"

America, in the endings from everyone's life, and in the beginnings of everyone's deaths, we complete, days of our country, from wars to create, three wars – overall in its –"World War Three." I, am in the American President's Warring' Office!"

This is the battle plan, for this "New World Order." I am on the side that wins. The battles and wins, to the point, from the Americans, would be whatever, from whomever, wins my war, or my – War Office!" For everyone, to "Follow The Yellow Brick Road!"

I am, Riley Miller! And I am, war's writer. In, this book of my work, I sincerely worked times and times, again, to simplify my philosophy from wars. It, is that war is good in the USA, for something, named all of us, as America's, followers of a Great World War!

America as in Antichrist of war, is timed as overtimes, in terms of a "third world war". To be in the shores of an American – wins!

Warring philosophy, of man whose words I am in the endings for warring times of my life. I won, over sentenced deaths, of soldiers, by myself in office, future from all, from the waging of "World of War III"", at work.

I, am in the beginnings, won are that from slavery, and of freedom's notorious voiced USA servants, made of the promised land of remade winning, from sold warring surmising, proclaimed peaces.

We as Americans, won of the beginnings, and in the office of wartimes, a world ally and a new worldwide humanity, will end, all of the days, of this war.

The annihilation of humanity, from what is
called the American third democracy's war! The
American Americanism automatic aged
weapons, are from wars, are over deeds, of
humanity's sold, battle-born, and American
armed, countryside, worldwide killing machines.
towards entirety of the armies sizes, seize an
American battled state, or Warring Superpower!

proliferation, of one man, "World War!"

war is on, and in this book, of declarations.
The war's independent and fighting book's sold
message is to recruit all Americans to world war,
of America's three, or, the American third time.
Instructions in war, of literature and powers!
This is on the manual, onto these powers, of the
insane book, in intelligence. Now soldiers, are
for war, become recruited, programmed minded
wars, from the fighting worlds, of America. The
third America, won over every Americanism's
started fighting, from the wars, and soldiers,
from the fighting, of the ancient times, of the
America independence, to win again, in our
nation's, "New World Order's Age!"

Only America, wins three wars. A new
ordered oneness, of a new professed birth
and admittance, came in the United States of
America, President's office. The President
Barack Hussein Obama, is the name, from
the America's, leader. In ages of war, and in
moldings the form from freedom, the lands
of America, participants from the model age,
is another third, world war's age. To winning

wars overnight, the careful planning of powerful sources, firstly knows America, and secondly; recruits worldwide USA, wartime's winning, dominating sides. The third aged, warring America, is of the American – "Third World War!?" The fighting of soldiers, the recruiting of soldiers fighting, then the soldiers of America killing, the US is fortuned, for peace!

"The USA!!!" The President of the United States of America, is the leader of the "free-world!"

The War Office, in is warring ordered plans of war, sides within the homeland, the other worlds, and the third age of the man – in New Order of the World.

I willed, to formed proclamations of justice, and decrees for freedoms, in wins over all, of every land, culture, and nationality.

Land firstly established as, "America's War!" The highest position of power, in the nation of, "America," is the President of the USA! Inside of war, in the intelligent life, of the foreign lands, and tested famed countries, and not lands on this surmising positioned countries, the best from the lands, is the free-world, of the USA, in figures of powerful people, and leaders, and positions of Presidents from other nations, we can, "Win WWIII!"

From our times, and the circumstances, from everyday livings, and unto another everyday dying, units of uniting, all of America, as leader of the third world war. Laws, measure and, spoken in word and in writing, a deed beyond, themed storied, world-war three, of the soldiers! Always, in deeds and works, the President of the United States, is elected in the public office, for popular vote! For the most impressive book, on war of themed office, concluded three worldwide wars ago, and announcing to bring – "World War Three!"

In the Office of the Chief of Staff, or the Presidential duty, attention to the plus and minus, of war, is of sides! Americans, always picked as only Americans, die to live, the greater life, that I hope concatenates the manual for war, in the hands of good personalities can defeat the evilest personality of, arguments of wars.

The third war, is mine before the Doomsday war, begins and ends, in "Nuclear War!" Americans, warring the battles, and choosing the world war, shall see a winning world, over what is evil, bind and ensnare, nationalism and democracy, over laws of our country! The Oval Office, the White House in D.C., and the Senate, House of Representatives, and the Staff of the American Presidency, is all summed up, to wars, even American, sided wins, defeating deaths the USA, way from life.

Strong willed, reading books, the High Seat of American roundtable, the hand and chair, is willing for the Christian leader, in choices to sit in the seat, in highest precedence of the one man's nation. The followers in parties, from American's national states, the USA, by one

choice of one voice in actionable chairs, from
Senators, supported side of laws, by matters of
deskwork, in conjunction of passing of the bills,
in wooden support, the President's chair, pen, in
hand, and the desk, opens, and closes, the door,
the hand opens!

Welcome home, Riley Miller, we should
enjoin to the fourth of July, of American beauty
of lands, flags, and stripes, of red, white, and
blue. To, on the risen pride, for the American
flag's, victory over all's World War Three, of the
American minds. The mind of victory, is from
the American flags. These, are freely flying!

To be in these times, is sad. I, want to know
more, about World War Three, in flags! These
are the surrounding, and the difficult times, of a
great depression? The polls are closed down!?

Duty, Service, And Honor of the Third
World War Times – Dedicated In Is Fullest Life,
Into The Biggest Star, In the American
Homeland.

A FREE-WORLD – FROM TEXAS, TO ENTERING NATIONS!

To Enter Into The Winning Sides of
Freedom of State of Texas Republic, Texas
Tradition, Texas Great and Big and Lone Star
State's, Honored Soldiers, The Tried and Truest
Birthplace of Mister Riley Miller –

The Texas Birthed Stars, In The Wynne
Family of Texas!

The Fame of Members, Miller Family, of Riley Miller's Fortune's Roles of All Trusted, And Official Families!

To – The Great State of Texas!

TO – THE "UNITED STATES OF AMERICA"

To – The United States of America's Presidential Roles, and the Representatives of the Oval Office From the USA Presidential Position, and the USA majority elected voting count, the President race for Office, from the Minority vote, the USA's Staff from workers in the White House, the USA Senate and its Represented Members of the US Senator Floor, the House of Representatives, and to Congress!

INSIDE OF THE MIND, OF MY WYNNE FAMILY!

The United States Presidential Oval Office, and to the USA Senate, of the House of Representatives, as my native Texan, lead role as life, wins as the Great State of Texas – "Wins WWIII!" From my minor role of writings, for wartimes' President, and above anyone elected, I have won it's all, and I've won, everyone in all three times, of the American war's, titled books!!!

I ask no to, other writer, as theirs in wars, of these comparing myself, to Prince William (Wales), from the people from who know my books! To the Electoral College, of the Popular Votes, for the – "USA Presidential Title!"

I, have won, the world's over all the forces, in this life, and so on, in the – "Life As Wins!" Or, the Wynne's family, from Dallas, in the Great State Of Texas!!

Alliance, of an impossible job, does to makeup, an official leader's role, in the third world war, of world war three's, persona, in the Trinity's, from Texas! A war story willingly told, of persons, in office representatives, World War of a third time, in Doomsday, Texan, in starry eyes! I wrote over ninety books, as in, written in an imagination book's world, of the United States people, of the American states. I cannot attest, ever being, for myself, I live in living, as Christ. As, good as gold, can I sit, and write in the best-ever, ninety books, of the mind's end, as happens the power at the end's promoter; as another literature writer's life, from a lifelong role of mine, in what I wrote, how as, a numbered list, of – "91 intelligent books!"

USA's Presidential life, in all the life's Bibles, as from an aged Kingdom secretly, indelibly planned, and hand written, as the books, on the dull life, of mine – "For An American President's Desk And War Office."

As By The Author – Riley Miller, As The Writer!!

(For The Reader)

As American, Right and True, Natural Texan – As An Christian And American New World Order's; Own and Loaned; "USA Presidency" – The Life From World of, "World War Three"!

Wartimes –

My Living Strong-Willed Persons, All Win War's Together, In Their Life's Games, Found Out Everyone In Our Lives' Business Deals; From Therein Politics Of Circles, At The Top's Wins Above Christ, Won On Popularity Votes!

All-Knowing God's Willing Texan State Republican, Christian of Churched Of The PCUSA, I Love Game of War's Books!!!" With Wins – In The NWO!

My Goal to Win – "The New York Times", Best-Seller's List!!! The – WWIII of the Dallas Morning News!

"My War's Willing Then Totaled Life"

By – President Riley Miller

One Quote As In
For World War Three –
(The Second Adam)

    The rebirth, of Adam, as my depicted soul!!!
The advent of world war three, is the fall of
man, and the reinvention of, the human man.
His desire, seems to be, to have the fallen
knowledge, of man. Adam, fell in the
beginning, then this will also, happen once
again. "

Chapter 1 –

All War Is Inevitable –

As of now, in America, there are winners and losers. The entire country, is of leaders who, run the world from itself, sited is in these times of need. In the Holocaust, of WW2, came Hitler.

From Russia, the "Cold War!" And the US, terrorists??? I, will not ever, forget – "9-11!" The whole world, watches. America is its friend. But, what happens in Antichrist life when, all nations are from – "War Evil?"

Will, all Americans, still live, their life, to the fullest? I, do not know, ask "Young Life!" Ask, "Joe White!" Ask, "Jesus Christ; Our Lord!"

In, the year of 2000, I saw Heaven. I saw castles. It is in a vision.

In, 2009, I saw the – "Antichrist." He, ruled with an iron fist, that is a – "666." He marked everyone. He was the mark. He, led us all, into World War Three! I, was in, vision. Now, I have an, "attitude." I think, I can lead, the American war.

However American wars win, and from the costs of war, Germany loses, the last battle. The Americans, in the costs, of the fairy tales, of stories, in the everyday life of mine, came from data. The data, from the computer, keeps records, of USA knowledge. The Illuminati, we all see, just watches, all of, the – "USA!" In world war three, I am the victor.

One day, I've seen all this data. All I did is,
"look". Then, what appears in USA data now
is, however the, "New World Order," became
mine, of the Illuminati, from America. I, now
will, fight for you, and I will win! The America I
knew is willingly mine! I, shall win, everyone
over. One day, I want to win. All of the world,
I will, this want, into winning. This is to belong,
to my, world will. I will join, the Internet's
Illuminati.

From this data, the illuminati, controls the
world. The entire world version, of World War,
is of World War Three. History's story is the
America's, "black magic". This enemy, I must
remember. It, Wars, itself.

The USA's Illuminati, and in losses, I, do not
know how, that World War Three, will ever, end
up as American.

I do! I know how! This is it! The world war
three; it will begin now. Show this battle, which
is an everyday battle, which it is, up to us, as.
To stop, the American tradition, from losing,
ends this confliction, of the American flag.

We all, in victories, must win. This war time,
just has to be, over wins. This country stands
the test of time. Eventually, our USA will win,
over all.

This stands up, and into alive in the new
aged, "USA People!" All, I know in this new
world order's time, is that we will win in, the
world war of – "WW3"!

Supporters, from the streets, of Babylon! All
nations, win the test of times! America is, to

solve all. Heaven, and Hell, knows. The world, and that of which tells, the story's entire plot! America, wins! If, of World War Three, then all will, win!!! I promised, all of you, only to this, factor – "to win!"

WORDS OF WISDOM

"To cause having life, to be from what America decides, there must be a war, and in its place, arrived in this place, the sides of good and evil, to overcome the injustices. Only, one winner!"

- As An American Fallen Soldier, I Fall Off The Planet's Edge – In to the, "New World Order!" The Return, To Earth, From Every Fallen Race.
- Riley Miller

From the American side, of this story is about, only wars. In the "Nazi Germany days", wars won. Histories, decide! Germany, knew this is about, how the American war, loses. That negatives, is if, all madmen, control the world. This is, from the new world order, and from America's losses. This country, wins with the New World Order. There, are peaceful states, of the order. The world order's callings, is to collect the collect call. Presidents, own it. Delegates, decide on it. And, America reacts solely, to itself, in laws.

Losses of the life from our country, all tell about the victory over God, from the lost lives that are, in the daily, wars and battles, and complete wars, of the world vision. A war, of

World War Three, is not inevitable, in the history, from Americans, but only true in foreign powers also. Only the good side wins.

The warring countries, in this time, are China, Germany, and Russia. The wars, at the endings of the days, are the Antichristian, Anti-American wars. They are counted, as God's Holy Bible, of meanings, that we cannot fathom, with wars.

They are the top dog's, biscuit, and bones. They, as Americans, are the top dog's, law abiding citizenship, and respected councils, from whom, lose the war. Never-ending stories, plagiarized, the Holocaust, as what the World War Two's, endings, condoned. This is, the moral of the story, which as of one Christian, in the world, I, have made significant, progress, in this life, and, in Heaven. Why Heaven, is only an idea?

In my life, I cannot fathom how life, on the Earth, is history's lie. Even Germany's, feared Adolf Hitler won, WWII! An autocracy so big, that from the Holocaust museum, the victims were wiped clean. The entire beautifully worked, tale of soldiers! An, entire country, became blamed, of victimized races. The Jewish, people were, so lost.

All, demands of his philosophy! All due to fallen times, what is historic, is due to the fallen knowledge, from the snake. Why is it in life that won over Jesus Christ and God and the Holy Spirit, why evil wins? Why, is it to everyone, in this war's pastimes, of death's life, and of this, world war three ship, comes the sinking sailors?

The man of history's life, that fame, power, and glory, cannot forget – 'World War Three!"

Some say Communist people, are victims, of World War Three??? Therein life peaces, is not eventually traced back, to America, as one country!

There, are also China, Russia, and Japan. The countries, of sin, are these countries. The Nazi Communists lost of World War Two. Their plan, from the Communists, is to make the whole, "new world order", only the enemy, as the country, of theirs to lose. The book looks good in ideologies, but the enemy's contextual analysis, is eventual.

The found life, from the underground, of America, eventually shows, its face, in WW3!! The version of life, for the poor, is starvation. The mad world, war undoes in America. The innocent, of counted lives, are hidden from countries. These treasures in Heaven are only, from an afterlife. Love of thy brother, lies from the heart to hell, spoken in tongues, hiding, what cancer is hidden in courts, of justice. The nicest world, of everyday life, is all gone. Just picture hands of history, made in liberty; on this title of war, from justice, in the US "Supreme Courts!"

Whoever is evil is dead? Whatever is in lying goes to jail, on Bibles? What costs of life? Whose surrendered life is made out of American history's freedom? Who is controlled by a false desire? Why, is to make God proud, in those whom loved, an evil life? Why is the best, of the best only, if surrendered?

Why is not, one man, always not to a false religion? We are definitive to the USA's fallen soldier, as to everyone.

If in worldly evil times, we win. In world war three, or Texas in true world wars! Why, is all those victims, came from, knowledge? Those whose image we reflect, as our fallen idols, realize war, as evil. Why is the fallen man of Adam, from the history of doubt?

Do, you really know me, or my evil in the thoughts? I know your living days, on then thinking lives, of your own, eventual thinking! I am not, why you are, the thinking man, of thoughts!

I have a good country. I have forgivingly, thanks Adolf Hitler, for World War Two. I must respectfully, wanted to bring this world, into the peace of the world. Go towards, the goal. Make my mark, and stand up, to be a, true hero of, "A Man America's tradition".

God came into the world. He desired to be, loved as every good American, are to be loved! So much happens in war, from that in one land, and in another lands, we still are fighting, clashing in sides, gone mad in wars. Freedom, is freeing, in the lands of war. History is one big, lie. In this history, there are world wars. In the life of mine, I believed in God.

In war times, we are all alive. We have democracy in life, and in this, living democracy. The life, of mine is freedom based. Intellect in power, control end and beginning, as freedom based, puppets. Puppets; are not the masters. That is solely, it, in wars.

Puppets are ours. People, will win wars. So will puppet masters, if they believe in us. Why believe in power? After three wars, we are exampled to win. Americans, to the raw power, directs why democracy, only wins, in world war three.

Sands of new times are covered, over the sands of ancient America, in the ancient aged old times. We all, arrived on earth, from an age old order, of the age of sold, histories.

Now, after old times, we've recovered. The new age ordered, of the man from the war. We, at these times, are already, at an age, of war. Following the ancient Freemasons, is the 'new world order," of man's, lost democracy. War, in the golden times, when democracy ruled the country, was in the Founding Father's story, of America.

Stories are told, from history's pages. To American's wins, which are from what history's wisdom affects, see in the eyes, of an old man. His worldly perspective, completes days, of wins from war? By the graces of one man and war, I thank, ancient times that were hard. All people have lived, in the ancient ages, on the display, at the history museums.

Forget, that in needy times, we are to be liked, in their religious persecutions. All, by the British Americans, on the war's terms. The absolute wartimes, countdown to doomsday, when Armageddon, happens, to innocent people. Why in wars, are wins only? To be just in fight, that is in fought, to win? In this, is our

America? The battles of Armageddon are not fought, to be won!!

The history is the best, at war! I still, have lived life, in its studied, nature! I sometimes, really cannot judge; of Jesus Christ, in whom, or is in God. The American soil's land, is into the chosen lands, as if we go, ask until I am going, onto war in American grounds.

Lands and seas, as if, we are counted in America's number, are in the wars, as is of lost or won victories. Our history, on open pages, is made of lands to winning sides, and seas, to winning countries. All will, win. We will win wars. The war's property, on winning sides, is from winning or losing sides, of the world over.

The history that we are in, is then land chosen. The playthings that we grow up with are gone, unless we win, over American's soul, in its entire all. The choices, in all countries, are on, whomever, are dependent on whom, have the winning sides. We, all love war. The land of the free, is not dead, but alive.

Due to wars, we are lost, in living. Three sides, to all winning, of three wars, are our, mark. I, want to make, a mark on man.

One person's, new world order!!! But, his is, the principle of this all, therein is into, the safety, of the country's life. If one country attacks, on America soul, as the fired shots, fights back, then in war's life, from these losing, situations, comes losses, from the President of the United States of America. But, if a President retaliates, he dies, themselves as countries die, and all hell willing, he breaks loose, over history's, all. The President, can be shot. This is the worst crime, in thinking's nature.

We always, must account, for all lost lives. The world's blamed, die off. The numbers, from times at hand, of individuals fighting in wars, came from wartimes, then come from history, as its pages unfold, from world wars. But, we are never the puppet-masters of democracy, or the puppets from abuse of justice. We are all soldiers. We, win wars.

In books, and inside writings, we exist as but just soldiers, of fortune. By, having lives, lost, soldiers lose, what are in lands needed, in times of war. The absolute winning side is America. I have sold this idea, to many people. The history is, from that which is being, on all the sides, of their justices, and is in lost countries, and the lost democracies, of America.

How we live, is in how we are to swim to the shores, together. As one, of the greatest American body of water, the Biblical Jesus Christ, walked on. Win its pride, and then I can make, these men, to the shores of history's America.

To win, in just a price, to pay, there is no cost of amounting, in deaths. Towards the day, when we win, three world wars, the hand of the ancient Serpent, or "Dragon", is covered. The United States of America's, best followers, are the United States of America's followers, and are in, the newly made loved life, of this life's living. Living creeds, which is to not ever help all people, is to help you, to all my riches.

My life is centered on Young Life camp's people. I row, in easy times. But, we are in hard times. Wars, are in this country. Deaths, in tomorrow's times, are to belated, irony.

When wars happen, the war's camera will film. The media, from the times of world war three, is how we will communicate. We, came alive past doubts, arrive of the countries of war.

So is talk, of the New Jerusalem. I, find out what this is, with Jesus Christ.

I am paddling harder. I am, knowingly, am increasing. Then I see the shore. In my boat, and with the more effort, I sail. I set sail, in the boat. I, am gliding across a lake. I arrive, to the shores. I, with my friend, cross safely.

On the other side, is the Earth's Heaven's, living, castles in the sky? I lived, a vision, in Young Life camp, of the "New Jerusalem." I saw my, Heaven! And, I am happy. I am just a man. I do not know how a man ever? I sailed, in a boat? I've, have had my visions.

My vision of my life, in this, is in what is, true as my Father's – "Friend!" Hell is within him. Shores on the other side, he carries himself, in the boat, to dry land. God wins, in my mind – "Jesus Christ!"

The America he sees beautifully is guaranteed his, as an ongoing life. His life history, form in the scenario from world war three, hates the worlds of hate. Here is the example, acting when this is, alive.

In and from, how I have fought, inside of the intellect of God, in the world, from wars.

Schools, all over the world's people, have
neglected young minds, and disregarded
teachers. And the goal wins in learning.
Whatever is another mission, of what I am in, is
from how I, came from, a new, another side, of
war. Americans lose. We, in all things, and in
olden times, are lost, in the media. The losing
of American values, in whatever, is in war's
mind, of Christ!

All deaths, win, in what is meaningless. Life,
is not, everyone's good. Choices and
opportunities in America are for men, in the
school systems, which get us started in wars. I,
see wars, with some of the greatest people,
seeking me out, as the winner of World War
Three. Was not that what, I was promised, in
this good life? What history, does not know, is
that war Generals, and are crazy.

As, life of, in a boat captain, and asks, what
might I asked not of his, then, he took his knife,
and then took his life. Sin, knifed everything, of
winning therein are not, worth living in, the one
and the not another situation, by the America
soil. I, have failed. I cannot mean, to lose, in a
life's – war situation. In my life, by and by, I
lose an egg. That egg is the life of me. That egg
is scrambled.

In, whatever I am gliding into as in, one man.
From whomever, he is faster in war. Lands are
his, then made faster. If, I loved, in an
American way, is it the ending forever, for my
life? War, is in these opened seashores, and
skylines of our country. I am paddling toward,
the ocean's edge, and Satan's war of Hell. My
hatred lives inside, too much thinking. I, live in

the traded life. One and only, America only
lost.

If only, I lived alone, then I would, in the
American tradition, dream the American dream,
and make American my home. I, love
successful, people. What make sense, in the
homes of mine, am me. I am an American
homeward bound, to live in this country. In the
past, nothing mattered. "I love America."

I've, lost myself once. In knowledge, who
dared from dream? Perhaps, toward the dream,
living consequences, is the third world war. His
love is to love a girl. If I, loved her. She is my,
Miss America, involving support, to her. I will
hold her dear.

I was my old girlfriend's friend, and a lover.
But, she was mentally, as an illness, was known
to happen to her, "mind". She was an
outpatient example at, an American mental
hospital, known as – "Hope." As, she fights to
stay alive, I must not protect and know her, she
calls herself, but she is mentally ill, at what
matters in world war three. Mass, I do not
know her.

In the American tradition, of forgiving.
Above the skyline, I've, seen all kinds of people,
in all ways, of life. This is my father's land. I
now cannot see dead people. In this life, and in
my last dying death, I cannot, die.

This is because I have Jesus.

Life, as is promised, not to kill you. The
meaning of man is in the American. He, knows
your life, and your death's plans.

Hell he wins, how he can fight a victory war, over you, and not, your happy lives. His, is United States of war, calling. Understanding is in war. He calls his father.

His nation is at home. He wins, and eats dinner, at the same, kind of meal, with the same, kind of people, as them. He, cares a lot, for the American tradition, peace is so much harder to maintain when you are high. The lands of America, from mine, are what is the chosen lands of the promise of the war, in the land of the free.

The home, of the American brave peoples, that I knew is free, is home. I like, to call America, home to, everyone. Wars are easy. If I start people, in world war three's ideology, all then, for a people win, a historic feat.

And as the forest's trees, hide. And, attitudes, on the boat glides, and as the reflection of the crystal castles, are what I stare at, and see, with a view, of Saranac Lake, New York.

My plan is to divide the American waters, with bad irony. I, have loved Jesus Christ, but I, always also loved, God much more! I have sailed the seven seas, wherein everybody is looking for something!

But as comes, what of nothing, but war, in my big life. I envision World War Two, like this, vision. In order to cross the shores and make it to the other side, I go across, wherein I go, and will go, swimming.

Nazi, Germany's Hitler's, becoming famous, came of war games. All wars were not war games at all, but examples of hate. Expenses in this free life, paid of queens living at the top, are not, worth this cost.

If I win, the war games from the top dreams, Jesus Christ, is in this life, as counted, then that is at all new world order. In, these expenses, pens are futile. The chosen lands, in the Holy Bible, were written of, by Moses!! He must win. He, saved the chosen, by parting the Red Sea. Water, is able to drown you, in the same way, that slavery is what, attempts to know, my God's, naturalistic nature. We are all, that which drown at sea, unless we are chosen, by the chosen by, History's God's people. What, if I am not? Life, in the land of the Promised Land that as not in Heaven, does anyone ever drown, but cannot is, by men, of honor as in who commit to – "Jesus Christ.

Some ever enter ingoing, that never again, from the shores of America, will I swim alone, perchance. In world war, I am swimming. As I may never go to sea, I will, not go alone. If I, ever again, go to world war three's, I will be prepared. My America is due to Jesus Christ. He is life, from the shores, in a foreign land.

If I can seek the American gold system, to see myself, crossing the lake, then I am a homebound person. To cross, the lake is my greatest desire, in life. If I, want to be myself, as I see the things, in war, all of myself, is then going back and forth, to the end world, of the new world order, of America's. Waters high, not going overboard, of the showing of the darkened waters, in the crystal life, of the story's past.

The colored rainbow, is in the sky, where Heaven and Earth, combine sides, is from what colorful. Colored, from one shore of beauty, as hand and hand, life wins by crossing the body of water, to make it to the shore. Across the lake, swims all of your life, with another, able-bodied person. I swam, across the water, to the Kingdom of Heaven.

God knows Himself. The loved war has itself, a God. If He loved war, then the entire world would be His. Life, fallen the same. And, from Jesus Christ, in little times, came along, in friendships, to lead the masses, astray. This is according to the American people.

American empires were lost, in the olden days. To, those who lived a life, I thank, every one of you. The person you are measured by is seen in court, as "always loved". For all, who loved you, as, my Americans, and in life as mine, some day, I will thank you, in the top-secret spot. Does, anyone read the Holy Bible, from God? Must I respect your choices?   In world war, we are sacrificed as lambs, in this frame, of mind to the USA, people.

Everyone, we all know about, talk about, how life, and war enemies, can talk. They speak, of world war's, plagiarism, in lost times. How the American, intellect and, smiling faces, of the lost America, and its everyday losses. We, lead over all, about the life, of the world war three, from an American perspective, of a natural war's leading, person. I am an American President, and as a person, I can see you. I can see all of you, and, then in this knowledge, and what is seeing what, in the world is about the world war three.

I am alive, in whose country, that this is about, is into the, "Mad World." From the shores of the Young Life camps, castles in the sky, I saw once, in the vision of mine, where I learned to swim, into the "World War Three," waters. I, have been, told that I, was a great leader. As one American, came to know as, an American mindset, then is of itself, in the knowledge of itself, who tries, this hardest to win!

Wins over what is in all, of America. Written philosophy, in books. The triple-sixes as a man! The false animal, in Revelations. The beast, dwells within hearts! Then, it is in this life – threefold. The Holy Bible, can be true. In words the accepts history, nations approval. Riley Miller, as a Texas, accepts legalism! The first, and last, step to the Antichrist, of American peoples.

Evil of mine. I knowing animal and man, in duality, of both sides, winning and losing, in world wars! War is in what it takes from presumably, the Antichrist, in who life, loses in works. The works, that himself takes on, to win the third world war, is asked, by only three men.

The three kings, of the Antichrist, or "tripled-six," man of numbers. On, my forehead history's war, is a six, six, six, mark! Threefold, on threescore of the number, "666". Marking the number of six-hundred and sixty-six, as three sixes, adding up to six-hundred and sixty-six, or three numbers, of the digit six, as one marks from the forehead! The sixes, of the numbered, triple-six digits of three sixes – "The Man of War!" In the Hebrew language, the mark identifies him. The Bible, understands him. The Antichrist, won. The Antichrist, and Christ, lives in! The soul, is the indwelling place, for their bodies.

Jesus Christ knows me. I, have been saved, by Jesus Christ. Christ, is not the Antichrist. The world, is for myself. This is if, I believed in Christ in three wars, of world war, three times. If, I can live, inside of these, deaths. Then, I would make amounts of banking, money! But, what does, not come from Jesus Christ?

In America, the Antichrist's America, and what is about me in times, and what concerns that is about the Bible, is of God. I can know that the world war happens, overnight with the Illuminati's, army of darkness, and army of goodness. And, from the American Dream, is the Antichrist, coming of the new world order, in the age that is from evil men, compared to all, we all will win, with Devil victories, but not in this lifetime's dreams.

My life, then is good. I am elected President, in what I am now forming of America, and in the visions of the New World Order, comes world war three. I can see, in which comes truest, in the America, of mine, wherein this war happens. Overnight, war itself is going to happen. My life is in going to World War Three, all is going, to be mine.

In itself, and from my life, came the life, and in I believed in, the American, of "World War

Three!" To demand in fact, about what is about these wars, in this book, that I win over all with, which is in from the writing, that is of mine. The real idea, behind of the American dream, is in the "Antichrist!"

America's whom is then going to war, to become crazy, as the American people. To follow the leader, and see what wins, we must follow the Antichrist of America, to see life. Then the America wins, in the third endings, of the third times, of the third world war, of the third person. The dream, of the American Antichrist, of wars comes true, in the life chosen, to the wars.

I, follow war's denials, of that event, which is so very crazy, that the situations, in how we react, are even having world war three, which sees wars, as the annihilation of the human race. The purpose from this war, in the life of mine, is to become the winner, as a winning part of America, as the war itself, moves on larger attitudes, and covers more land, than the previous ones.

The work from this book seems like a real story, which is all for the crazy life, of the war. In a war, in terms of Jesus Christ, there is a God, and a Holy Ghost, in another war, of world war three. This is because of America. He is the Biblical Antichrist. He has a thought disorder, which tells us this story. The story, came truest, of one war. He, is so evil, that he is crazy, from the evil, even from Babylon of the Holy Bibles. He is even, considered evil, by God and Jesus Christ. This is how, the war was told to me, by my father.

In the End Times, there is one fact, in America, that is true. This is that there is a, "World War Three," and, it wins. The wisdom of one man is in the Holy Bibles, as a Bible verse. It warns, of the Antichrist, of the American, "World War Three."

The stories, and the new world order, can come together, to form thoughts, of the truest, kind of thinking, of man, in the kind of war, we all loved. The New World Order, that is always American, is in the "One Man", who is also in the Third World War, as its, "Leader of the Free World." He himself fights in the American wars, and He wins. And, to cut the hand off, from the arm, that is also, another factual existence, of war.

This all came, from the world wars, that all are in the Antichrist's America body, and in how the Great Prostitute, leads it. Inside Texas, from the city of Dallas, in the state of Texas, is a, world war three, amounts to people. He is the evil one person, of World War Three.

I came from, into what is in the makings, of the American dream, of World War Three, in Texas, and in the story's tales, it is us then, that wisdom explains. In the language's title, of this book, is for what as is the message being delivered, and in the ways, for the wars, we win, that are the inadvertently wrong way, as the message to the public.

In this life, of hopefully seeing war things, that come apart, as the story unravels, there is the one man army. The ideas are closer, to the end, as much as each penned man, in what is written, that has the joining problem, of one man, of World War Three.

The mind of God warns, of the Antichrist. In Holy Bibles, and in what are simple, as in the warring sides, of the wars, are in themselves, which are the ways, of the wars, of themselves. What, is meant of war, in what to all means, which life is from itself, in this life, from themselves, as war Americans.

When, data strikes the interception points of life, of the triangles, and then forms the wisdom of a man, then people win, strategically. Wars come from that which forms the philosophy of war, as is in creating the life deeds, of the war, itself of killing, in many different forms. Ways, of a soldier's life, and then from this march to the end, begins from Dallas, Texas, and then goes to where the grown men play, a war game. In Texas, in who wins over enemy warfare is what is involved, in the business, of the war games.

What seems to be in this story, is the Antichrist, and was a young man, which I've met. In this life, I've liked him, and he sought fame, and glory in this life. He was in the Dallas, Texas, part of the family that was at the party, of the Texan Wynne's, family.

I, am from the Wynne Clan's family of, four hundred members, in the – "Great State of Texas".

The mathematics are the strategy in my life, from the participant's life. His name comes, from a soldier's tales, and of madness. It is important, to know, that we win. As madness,

there is as, war. Past the lands, of time, dwells
the understanding, of one man. In, his USA, in
this age, world war happens. He is the
Antichrist. He is in Bibles. The world, of the
American from the Antichrist is all for, himself.
In the Biblical Revelations, he is one evil man.
He, is not equal to the six-six-six, he carries,
around on the mark on his head.

The man, who wins, wins after a cause. He
must establish it, in the intercepting of deaths
over wins, which is in, American life. That is
the President, of the USA! His story is the best
story. His life is important. It is the story-line.
American deaths, only lead us, to time. Inside
of lives, his winning lives, that is as, he speaks in
tongues. He wills speaks, to the cost of man, in
– "World War Three!!!!"

People, are like the damned, attacked
civilizations that is in the, "Antichrist World
War Three". The data, formed as lines from the
interceptions, came when the wisdom, is of one
man. He marched, and created all, of this life.
Then, this was in the fall of man, from the kind
of the "First Paradise", that was the – "Garden
Of Eden".

The Third World War is not predicted, yet.
We all, do not know history, of our world. In
stories, all speaks of the Antichrist. The Bible,
American Antichrist is the man, which is in
these ends times. No one knows how he is to
come. The person, sure of himself, is an
American. World War Three is the war he
fights. And, he is coming soon.

To endings, or the man of the Armageddon, of a world war three, is of just one man. He is coming from, Texas. The man who is living from the other men, is from our, "New World Order!" The one man gives orders, to all men. This is how, world war three, happens. He in the newspapers gives us all orders in America.

The one man, he is evil. America is marching triumphant. As the songs from the soldiers, made sense, we march. In, passing to safety, we win, the created life, from wars.

All came from wars. Life is in none of what I can feel. Mighty honestly, is in waging wars. Inside of the mind, what the war humanity, does. Losing, sides. For, in ways which cannot be intercepted, as losses, we win. Nonetheless the powers to be, unless, the day as the knowledgeable world, is accept evil, then all will lose. American lives in history, that soldiers marching, and going to wars, is allowing heralded and working in wartime of small and to the big.

He, as God, came from all evil men, unless interpreted, in truth. We, form our actions, to be, what we are, "America's Public!!!"

As tried and true, no evils can accept man. In wars, no one wants, to win, from the intelligence mind's ways, of Communism, to be only from, the standards, from evil men. They come in from pirate ships, and destroy our nation.

The living wars in this life, within the evil men, are all of, "World War Three." Sand in eyes, explains why he and she, is evil, in this war. We, are that the triumphant soldier's march, that is of the Antichrist. If I, accept the American war, of third time, thus as the American President, I can explain this action, to duty. It is simply the fact, that from what America is, thus I wrote down on papers. Therefore, war as soldiers marching, is then in this book! I wrote down World War Three's, main strategy.

But, of it seems as if war, exists, than so do the killing. There is in mind, the souls of the lost, and innocent people. If at all, one day, we lose?

Would we, if this really was the true, war? My life would continue on as the greatest. Only my version would be accepted. Heaven's Jerusalem, is the final destination, of this winning, from my acceptance, only in war.

Then, in hatred of a mad man, is alive. Lands of opportunity, of his vision came out. Golden trees clogged his mind. So now, he sees. He really, in this life, is not one of Americans. We learn, from the Holy Bibles, to serve. But, in that act, but himself; Adolf Hitler was this madman. He, is the example. We, have learned from, our past mistakes. Our wars, came from the common sense. We are of ours, as the Americans. We all, shall will, the wins, of our Country. And, then we would all, celebrate. In

Christ, we who that wins, over all worlds! America, if now, as herself! She – could see? America, can win.

The Antichrist, or he, who in this life, wins over all of his wins? We all, win then. Third wars, of the world war three times, if in wins of ourselves, can we know justice? His anarchy, replacing by justice, is known through killing the whole wide-world.

With the wars of the worlds, phrases, and highest intelligence, all wins. Americans, can create the designed, of a circled life-form, that forms the shaped, loved deaths. The world war three, as the dying aged of man's victory, won. We are from deaths. They are the pasts, of the wartimes. The systems of wars, of the better man's philosophy, can enter! We enter a third time – "From Myself!" Americans, enters into world war.

Marching soldiers, into the unknown, rapes the USA! From national freedom, is the soul. Nations, of the world wars! Our versions are complete in the arms of America. War's soldiers, are those who end in the evil ways; lives of humanity. Then, this all, makes sense, to Americans.

The triangle death, and the circle life, takes shapes. "We are alive", to form illumination, in this, form today's wars!

Who in, the American world, sat and stood, one day? Who sees, from the world offices, a persons' big chair. Persons of – wars!

New World Order, wars, is personally growing as today! Faster and faster, onto the mostly thinner world wars, was what formed, a life. Will won, within the war's front lines. Me, as in what, schools created. By must, of what comes, the victory of the created lifelong victory's standoff, then wars of, all the wars, can happen to be, only America's, from Ancient pasts. We, wins.

The tree's life, with the ripe apples or oranges, is on trees. To, who lives a life, as an apple. It also dies from death. The supportive tree lives, as if, to please. And, when it dies, a person, can benefit. A tree, is for human, pleasure. That is to why it lives.

And whenever man fell, it was from the tree of life. The temptation, of the tree, was too much. As is, in wars!! As living is as dying, knowledge does, all. In trees, there lives life. In this tree, there came temptation. All knowledge, in war is, a cost. You, live either or you die, for what you are, is in how you can live, for your country. Why wars happen, due to knowledge, as in how came thieves, made from the form of Adam and Eve. The fallen world, was stolen, due to the disobedience, of one man, "Adam." All wars, of the greater designed natures; wisdom! Came, from Adam in the fallen knowledge, from the apple of death's construction!

Life of the wars, always in death.. The shaped and formed nations, came from apples. Wars came from what the followers, are to seek, in what is American. From past lifetime's apples, are the times ripe with knowledge?

Actually war, is what an illusion, from knowledge is. Death of life, in what are designed from the wars, as from wars – "Is America!"

Thoughts of killing, is in life. Knowledge is as simple as the, illusion, as a tree. Whatever wins, trusted lives over are as is much, as God hated the Tree of Knowledge.

That is the reason, of the third world war. The double-edged sword protects the Tree of Life, in the Holy Bibles. The Tree Of Knowledge, came from – "Deaths!" That, was God's, curse on the human beings, from the life of the Garden of Eden. He, cursed us all, with death. That, is to why, all living beings, die.

The Tree of Knowledge was the tree of death. New deaths in wins, form as the appearance of God's will, as man fell. Cursed the world, from deaths from Adam! As all we stand, within circles, and the illuminated shapes, from the trees of life in forms of knowledge, came of the world war three's, soldiers, to die for our countries. The world will lose world war three.

Today, in that world, are what war three appearance of life, the fall wins, from knowledge. That is what, is in World War Three, caused losing deaths to other people. In masses, in what is from chaotic masses, we are as destined for victory! Lives lost and a life found, is what, came true, in death from the appearance of war. The natural selection, of the World War Three Office, of the President of the USA, costs deaths!

Three times, is the triangle, from one rounded, new world order? The circles, and squares, do take shaped, in this lifetime trilogy, of God's third world wars, entitlement.

The light within, in this guiding light, is life. The wisdom, can intercept what the living wisdoms, of prophets, can do and say, in world war three. The guiding shape, forming of new illusions, which can start now, can know questions of every, kinds of life. The book, is the simple explanation, that as from how, we die. But, to live, from the wars forming lives, from the Dallas, Texas, family? The three world wars, live in this illusion, in the story tales, of the fighting, in the New Jerusalem. God?

Welcome home to Texas, to the Great State of Texas, for the world war three's system, of the design, of the popular forms. The standards of wars, from one man to another whole man's catastrophic, versions of life, arrive to, the inherited in man. He, thus all came, for the Antichrist. He is this winner, from the war, as knowing the good and evil. Today is gone, from man, now and then, from what happens, to us. Watch me learn, as if the Americans, at world wars, were in the starvation of the planet; that comes in – "World War Three!"

These wartimes, that we know accentuate, what are the thoughts, behind the third world war! It is the intellect from America, behind the thinking, of a man. And the fighters of the war's thoughts are the very actions, from evil wars, of Capitalism. Natural ways that are not actions, but are in, these lives of the American Antichrist, of WWIII – extinctions from deaths?

But why are we living? Why, are natures big to win, over all themes, over evil winning in – "Antichristian America?"

What happens, from today's standards, of the minimal costs of today? Why, in capitalist designable standards? Waiting, from the expositions, appear of life, in what is in the light of the ways, of the exposure's lives, in the ending of times, from wars, as all won?

Toward the seeing designs, from whatever is clear intellect's, in what knowledge, from the mind that the most people love, of these American powerful families, wherein these choices, are from the peoples, as to who finds out. What it, is intellect of the unexplained. I knowledgeably can, alone can, ever feel that I alone as myself, and me only, in wars! What happened when life's happiness; lost! I, never have fought; for all evils.

America, in what there is, must be a new age started. Of one life, as all of the third time's war, as first in what begins today? Now communism, in a third world war, wins then from first win, and continues, to all of their world war three's, derivatives, that skills to win the war, are none.

Intelligence from our humanity's core is from, living. American great slice of the American pie, is how, America wins. This is, to the equality that means nothing. If no life's edge, and in wars, to that meaning, as nothing is at equality, then in this life, death does win.

Apart from God, then enemies will lose, to the higher powers. All, of war, does win! Then success, and I and, "Ourselves," from our wins, will find intelligence, from wars. Intelligence from books, are the people from wars, and the wars and the lives, within hell, in what came from people which, we lost to.

We all lost battles, to the Holy Bible. If we do rely on Satan as our master, then America is, lost. How wrong! Why, in wars, would a nation, sell our soul? If, creating Satan, is the evilest act ever, we as Americans all must learn! He, always is our enemy. In the distance, farthest away from God, in the good people's loving life, there lies another – "one world order!" This time, it is warring sides in end days, in everyone's good America.

In war, of the churched living spaces, are the places of the God's interesting, and most loving people, who do no wrong, and do not follow World War Three. Following the hearts of Satan is known as, what are impossible. Into the measured distances to war, contradictions are from the problems, to account for dead lives, in the world wars, which are surmising. There is no future, with what is not, in what people's pasts, really are.

But, missions from what militaries want, is now as world war, and but what is in the future's lifetime, which does not matter, and does not amount, to anything? We live, our lives as to live well. But what really is in what the world war's, strategy, really wins! Covering all peoples on every nation, within all men, thereof, in counting the evil men's plots and problems, against what, came as American's, nations.

We as Americans? Why, are we not all equal, in other countries? As Americans, we are in living this life, which we are not all equal, in as a contextual, life in happiness. In America though, is a greatest force of the life, if there is no one of American equality, then there is no fun experiences. Life exists in, differences from deaths, which are in the middle, of living freely. Do, not put death in the middle, of this free-willed life, that sins in war. It, will survive, on its own, like it never did, in the enemy – Nazi Germany.

In three world wars, there are three nations of elected and equal people! We are in wars! Now we are all, as are God's, equals? Then, in the Trinity of God, is the saving of souls. War's won worlds! How sacred life, saves the souls, of the people. As another form, of it! As, a war's third time, as an office, in an office, I am a sad man! This only- "War!!!"

Whatever, if what this man is, that the man is – "Barrack Hussein Obama." The sadness, or enemy, of this office, is that the Presidential Office, man is – "World War Three!" We will miss your, life and death; – "Mr. President Barrack Hussein Obama!!!" We will now know, that love is war, and war is loved. We will choose, a new American nation, of American war-times, for nationalism. To wage war, is to gain, allies!

My America, in world war three's, office! It is excellence, in why that, is to the American nations! Lives in what costs, is to win over all evil. This is gradually, in this lifetime.

The lives, from the unknown, are simple explanations, from myself. Warren Buffet, a billion dollar man, is well worth; all. Trials, are insanity, and are from what, angels do. Fallen angels, denied happiness followings then mattered to men, is what are too simply put down, as an insult to continue, to be mine. The – World War Three, appears to be mine.

All, in the Holy Bibles terms, are from – "the Antichrist."

I've really literally, wanted to write in this book, to be like the President of the USA, behind the notes, behind the Cello, performing beautifully. Behind the wars, there are always a political office, seeking out, the victories.

Our own thoughts, if I could war, be a won US President, from a war office, in Texas. The Texas, Republican Party, from our fathers, in your American dream of war, makes us upon the hill of all, the seat upon the tops of the dollar, of the new world order, that reinvents itself.

Followers, came into the followings of the new world order, and the, "Man of Sin," who wins, in that recruiting way, who recruits America, with private working, men of war.

I am, that in which, in followers, in wars, in which, arrived and came as himself, wherein I am – "The King of the New World Order." How history, lies in the senses, that I do care, from all the fights of the world, of the Americans, which were, made to be, in history's pages, afterward wars then, count me in, as I am, Riley Miller.

The world war's times, are exampled in the book, in what are the prime examples, as to what appears from life, as to be towards people, who begin to see, just are what is to a greater method, from war's madness. These shaped ideologies, to the formations of the front lines, of world war three, which are the asking from which is, Antichrist America.

The methods, from the "men of madness," came out of the Texans, whom think of the American philosophy that was foretold in Holy Bibles. Americans, from the antichrist age, begin first and last, as coming from life. The acts, from being in occupied Bibles stories, from the American approached circle of life, we'll win.

The standards of living, in one voice the greatest meaningful life, is an American war, life. One man, whom of which is, now! The Antichrist arrived into Dallas, Texas. The strategies and plans, from the war of the third world Texas, is of the third time's wartime's life, and from firstly started versions of world war three's death's construction, is what book's were mine.

The lived as the extinct plans, of as all of the people. The war's demising, has to be what formed from the philosophy of the world itself. The one American man, for the American self, of me, as a complete as him in forming nations, is gone. Always, Antichrist America, wins of the World War Three demise, over China, Germany, and Russia.

The exampled life, from the thoughts, and formations of the circled shapes, vie from victory. These won wars, do not happen the world's way, but from world wars, from the third time after Adolf Hitler, we tried the American world war's times. The example of winning and waging wars, of the message, is not American, but anti-terrorist. Only from wars, is there no war, but from who is around the world, who supports it.

Go to the USA, of the world war three's coming, and find who, is the Antichrist. No one person, from the biggest American world war, can defeat him. He, came in the coming, from the peace of fame, in Bible's characters. He, from another wonderful war, that begins soon, starts as the bigger American soldier! Texas, then ends in the destruction of the whole world.

The life, within my dreamed, times ago, from the age of madness, is in a world, of present in times. As all repeating the history, I then purpose to the Great War's, no solution. The American soldier fights, again, and again, and in the world wars, carries life, on into the future. The, "Third World War's," theme of written works, is their, first and last, themed book. Books, of mine, are which is very read, and very popularly sought as in war, are the cleverly genius written.

Take careful notice for attention, in world war three's democratic state, in what is if consideration from the books is needed, pray then, what you read. In America, this is from God. In God's country, whatever you read in the books you choose, no matter, which

chooses it, America wins. Books, also win. As,
I believed in God for your country, and any
public person accepts it, we win together.
Always, if willing and able persons, can willingly
see, a be a part of, wars to be, then in the Holy
Bibles, is a powerful message of God.

The war's, generally made readers, won. Of
this book, from the history's living legends, like
Generals, Presidents, and World Leaders, of
whomever win wars. In US history, is an
officially new world order's book in the
chapters, in what are coming from what, is the
instruction book. The words are repeated, to
strengthen you, and to seek in history, what we
shall find. History's pages come from
symbolism of old wars, which is in wars, from
only one man. From history's legends, in which
leading the USA's masses, and killing all of the
armies, of the other country, is the USA goal,
from the antichrist. How, then do they lose
and, then go away.

The circles of the world, with the war lines,
are soldiers around the wisdom, of man. He
circles life, of the worldly, craft. These wise
thinking, from the thoughts of man, exist to
please God's wisdom, as it is in and of every,
"one man". All, American wars, have been in
the past life, and has been from what is formed,
in and around wisdom. That catastrophe is
wisdom.

Thanks to the reader, from the "new world
order", as an ancient order, can guide you to the
truth, of the followings, of the world war three.
From wars, of all times, you will be interested.
Examples follow through, in the lines that are

reading, to us. These world war, are the wisdom and excellence, of what I have seen! The Antichrist of America, with all the nations of people, and as followers of everyone, I see in the vision, of the whole world? Yes, following parties, in the circled triangle, going into world war.

The actions in life, and of the dead, are of world war three, from what is from this book. Thanks be as, to all men, and of my readers. Wars, from what this Antichrist, as seen is, in as what takes, in American shape, what is from winning. The one man, circled in shape, as the "Tripled-Six." That evil man is that man, who starts what is this worldly war – "The World War Three." I am, to begin, to win in wars. Wars come from my life's greatest philosophy, of reading.

This is of the war, of people itself, seeing victory marches, in itself. The American man, is the Antichrist American man's lives, beginning to, begin supporting saviors, of the world. The human coded designed standards, is yours to keep, onto the pages, in this books. Not, only in my life, there is war. But, also in wars, if America lost, then the end of the world would happen. I am the believer, of the American tradition. If, the circled terms, we all fight, and for the American's armies, in the wins from wars again, and wins, of again and again!! We all, are!!

RILEY MILLER

Chapter 2 –

MY WAR'S MOST UNITED
AMERICAN DEMANDS

WAR – WINS!

However in the United States of America, In It's Lost Wars, Do Even Americans Win, Over All?! Into, The New World Order, From the Totals of Upper Constructs, in All the Costs, Of the Third World Party, Come By the Word Of Mouth, And, In What Comes From the Outsides – "The Third World War's!" The song of freedom.

From – "The Third American Nation's Wins"

World Order, Ally People Win the First Placed Position As Ally, Of the Endings for American Imaged Mankind.

MY WAR!

From the Biblically Antichristian America; We Win!

We Come, All From the Unknown Soldiers, of USA'S Pastimes –

In The Days Office's, Off The Presidential Wartimes!

People Arrives all Over the Messages from the Holy Bible's Revelations, At the Destined Predestined Christians, And the Electoral Parties, Into the Futures, Of All Wars, By the Elected Presidents, From Them In Church.

Every Nation For The American President of the United States from America, Enter Except Riley Miller, Into Itself, in World War Three?!!

Why My National Ideology Of All-Knowing Peace, Shared Actually All, But Nothing to War.

I Willingly, Accept the President Bid, From the United States of America.

As Is, Another New Formed Ideology of the USA World War's —

In a Front Office, War As In World War Three In Ways, From the Soldiers Forming Lined Marches, To The Planning From The American New World Order, of War — America Wins These Endings From Times, Of the Enemy's Status —

RILEY PARKER MILLER'S WAR

In Thinking That to Chosen Armies of Darkness Rule the Global Elite, Then from the Willing Ways of War, That All Is That Knowledge, That in People, World War, Does Win!

What in Life Can becomes in the Surrounding Areas of the World, from the Third World, Of Peace? America, will win, and gain — "The One World!"

Wars, that in Fighting, in the Status Quo, of the Americans who wins, as another new President's idea. He, can come well-enough alive, to start the official, World War Three.

If I Die, I Know When Entering into the Laws of Humanity, Then If We Should Be

Respected, in the Destiny of the American, World! If, World War Three's People forgive me, then I am saved?

The American, Won All Over the Ways of Wars.

How in World Wars, Then It Is Done, In This Willing Point, To Be Of The Killing Of Innocent People?

Microsoft Word, From a Never-ending Plot to Rule the World, By the Antichrist. Is itself in, what is all to be mine, from all of mine, in the world war three's scenario, in society, of differencing?

I've, not knowledgeably learned, as because, of Buttered Toast, There Is None, Of One Duty, First Intelligent Only Leading World War Three In The Antichrist– This is But, One Country's Laws Involved, in Our Peace. If I Sell, These Are In These Laws, My American Man, When Has Every Soldier's Armed Units, and Then Allow There to Be Peace!

I am not the Devil's Advocate, of a person, who I am not like, in my life. I am, in the great looking family, of nice relatives, from the Wynne Family, In Dallas, and From Texas.

The Beast and The Antichrist, is in the Holy Bible. These dinosaurs, are extinct. The Tyrannosaurus Rex, is extinct. The Prehistoric Age, is an example, of death. The age of the new man, now! The Dinosaurs, like the Beast and the Antichrist! I, do not win. Therefore, is extinction.

I HAVE FALLEN. I FELL DOWN HARD. NOW WHO HELPS?

The enemies, we can become extinct, as seeing them. One, by one, the world war advocates, is preplanned, minds. To get the gist, sin is in the wars from life. They are the soldiers, ending the world. The world of newness, in made-up, lives are nuptial by the, "evil" The soul, of the evil? The mind, of humanity, Christ!

The friends in this duality, of duality of good and evil. Friends landed, on evil! Good, was decided! Plans are, in what came the intellect. The humankind, that enter from laws.

All, is in born into, the fears. In alive, new world orders, came are, of each person, the truthfulness who is in charge of the ways, of my own, in life!

For the; "rich", to form the life from humanity, is the Monday's blues, when you do not want to rise, in dawn. The mind's approach, invents of the world, instinctively from what tries, "a game of trivial pursuit"?

Wars allowed, from over God, is in America. The "King!! The sword, pulled from the stone of, impenetrability. The King, then defeats, the "Dragon!" He, gets all of, this gold.

He allows the hands of time, to end! Knowing that he casts frowns down upon, on my destiny, to be this – "USA?" Who, kills the antichrist?

In my life, and onto the world of wars, that if there are three wars, by one man who started one and finished one, to the ends of the American thoughts. Into, what it in war is, as the "New World Order", in what is from asked questions, if it is the way of the American, on top of these, top-notched ways?

I am of the new world order's ways into the days of every kind of everything which ends, but to fight in a war, is worth to risk your life for your country. The wars are in the days, of the tragic plots, and the losses, from one nation, of our nation, – "Our Nation!"

Confusion, about the started, "Antichrist," is of the, "God's Bible." I can know the things that are, way ahead of my time, and my publicly known image, and the places of vision, of where in this life, we are, there will be a world war three. Not one person can see, from my knowledge of wars, and what it is, within what God, has done, is a true life, to others, but in God.

Not even I can think as a person, as to think into the American dream. I am doing and saying, whatever another, man thinks, and, says in his life. In wars, there are failed, the war songs. These songs, that can appear, will appear. I can see the Antichrist, with the knowledge, of the "666". I can see now.

I am scribbling the messages on the chalk board. I am an attitude-adjusted, and a very special and clean, and sober person. I still can see and know how, of what I now know, and can hear of the overheard duty, and, as if ask it happens, then is when of the New World Order, if WWIII happens. If so, then Biblically, there will be Americanism, in the wars, of our home front in – "America".

How, the God's Holy Bible, in what came from my own creation, as in Riley Miller's, Holy Bible's version, of the last books, wherein the ending, of the holy books, "Accolades I & II," then all of revelations and from prophesies, and in visions, appeared in my NIV translation. The task at hand, in which is of a Holy Bible Book's remembered book, which has the versions of it, how of the versions, of the Holy Bible, in itself, in what has, from the ending of the books, of the Holy Bible, is God's Message, to the world.

The "End Times", in the Biblical Words of God, from the Antichrist, or "Son of Perdition", or the "Man of Sin", and a, "One-Man," ending the world, then it has war in the messages. In the Book of Life, and from the Biblical texts of old, that have inscribed money in it, and as an approving in God's message, there is the Word of God, which brings us riches. God knows, that from wherever, I've been, that is known, then He knows, even in what time night is, in world war three, even in victories, we will see, and to be, in these times, from World War Three, the promises.

These endings, of war, then is near, and is in world ended Biblical times, of the Holy Bible's, messages and the waging of wars, due to Communism, and of Socialism, and of the ideology in this America.

The "Anti-Americans," words in the believed in ideology, in from what the world's war attitude, will be like, as America wins over all. "If, I do well, I can win World War Three." "Of mine, then is yours, in World Wars." And, "All will do well, in the Antichristian, "Three World Wars."

The Third World War, as to what is in America's world, at this traditional life, that has life, in the ending of all, and in wars. Seems as if, we can find, and all people try hard, to find, themselves, in the war of the end of the, "New World Order."

Then everyone, should beware, of this "triple-six," the forehead mark, symbols as the mark of the Beast, and the Antichrist. The "tripled-six," is not, on top of this forehead, but is in his Biblical mind. The number, on this forehead, if we needed some clarity, is what it seems to be, as pure evil. Ask me how he, as seeking the number himself, from the Antichrist, that appearing on our forehead, in life, as we are controlled by him, and by the identity of the, "Son of Perdition".

I, can in the thinking only of knowing and cancelling of the doubt, and can have bittersweet remorse, if I possess, of the Antichrist, it can be, lived within himself. My living and breathing knowledge from these times, I placed a halo, on top of my head.

Spiritually I was connected, to the churches, to the alliances, and to the countries.

If I was, thought in my life, whatever I was thinking, into the knowledge of the Antichrist, and when of then his identity, as was occurring overhead, wherein I sat, we Think Of Destroys America! And As We Know Of American Life, And As the Savior of the World, Can Explain It, Of How The Man Or Tripled Six, is for my Starts, of World War Three!

And The End of America – "World War Three," is a new beginning in history. It does in fictions, the war and death, of times of trials and tribulations, in the end of the world, of there existed life, of the Antichristian knowledge.

We are people, at the third world war, where peace exists, foreign and domestic, of our America, of the Antichrist tradition. However in controls of the One Man's armies, in America, on showing us, the Antichrist, in what does the knowledge worth, dying and living lives for, ever attend to the new world order. Ourselves, in wealth from what I, really want, is and was, to have this, in this life, of wealth. Wartimes, should not only see, what won that is in American wars!!

Chapter 3 –
The Knowledge from War –

The laws of the Antichrist, as an approached
to explainable new world order, that as to attend
to the general unions, and the United States of
America, as for no one elemental doubt, and

from arriving into chaos, what happens is, in the
end.

In that the new world order has some
execution at another, commanding situation
over, another way, therein is the American
freedoms. What is, at this life from whenever,
in humanity exists in apprehending the life's
body, as it was, the humanity killing.

What occurs, in the Biblical Antichrist,
formation from its only humanity that as killing
is from and in the name of God, if it is as
American? The Biblical Antichrist or one man's
America, is in the adjusted individual life's
appearance, as an invisible character, explains
why chaotic meanings, can as happened, at the
shape of an annihilating impulse. Why, does
this happen, with in world war three?

The Leaders of the Bible to attesting laws, as
wins as leaders of the evil world, that people are
into World War Three, in God's world, as the
Antichrist, is Who Comes From The American
Underground Society.

He appears in the state of Texas. And
acquired intuition as applied, As the Attested
and contested to the explained moreover
situation, is formed in the knowledge, of the
world way from the Texan man, from what has
in, as support in fact him of him, is true war's
bloods.

His closed acquisitions, in which seems Of
Another Modern Day Stated Affairs, As Of The
Official Memberships To The New Aged Order,
As The Old Age, As The USA Itself, And
Intelligence of The One Man, Or The "Triple-

Six," is now apparent in America. He is the Better Living Human Being, in attested form, on the world war grounds, From the American genuine forth, of coming excellence.

The Founding Fathers of an American Antichrist Agenda As Is From My Life As A Member of An Official Group Of The New World Order – Known To Only Be As The Brotherhood Of Death – In However World War Three Will Be Won

The American Democracy's initially Stated Fact, As Relied on the Secrets, Of The New World Order, In The One And Only Fact, That The Antichrist Wins, and the New Age Continues

Nationwide Treatment of the President Came As Of The United States of America, Of The President, Who Came As A Surmising Bold Win, Of WWIII

The New Appearance of the New World Order Happens Overnight – Much Like The Treatments Of The USA Americans, Who Have Learned To Love To Lose

Freedom Will Carry On, As Unknown the Soldiers of a New World One-Government Order Continue, And We Won; The War!

The Presidential Questions Shall Arrive, Much As The Stated To The Questions That Whenever All, Over The World War Three's Victory and Arrival's March, When Orders To All USA Citizens Shall Start To Come, We Will Have Won.

As This Texan Times, We Eventually Wins! Then We Will All, As One Will Be As Who Becomes Prepared For World War Three, At Home

Then As For My Life, The New Aged Order Of Faceless Mercenaries, It Will Appear In The Doomsday Device Way, Known As The "Atomic Bomb," Will Wipe Clean, All Of The Natural Impulses and Make Clean and Ready a New Nation With A New Chosen Population, To Undergo A Change of Places, From "My Life!"

As History Known At Warred Universal War Beings, At World War Three's Antichristian Ways, Are In New World Order Warred Jews, Gentiles, and Christians.

I'm Three In One, All Three In God, for World War Three From The Trinity

Land And How The Senator's Powers and the President's War Office of the United States – From Them Knowing Already How To Protect Us All Of World War Three

Of However In Life's Helping Hands, We All Come, As Americans, While Others From Countries When They Play Another Attributed Part Or Role, As If In Texas, Ask In The Whole Lives, And Of The Lands Of Freedoms

Who Wins Wars, From This Role Came Into The Third World Wars, Of Trials And The Tribulations, From What As Become As Independent And At Intelligent Life From God, In The Triumphs And The Victories, We Played An Important Life Part

I Began, As For Where As Whom In One We
Win, All Shall Win As The Trying War Games
That Happened To End Times Of All Over As,
The People In America That Do Things To
Exist, We Win As One Whole World War

I Learned Life, From In How Life And How
All Of The Americans Had To Come Together
– Lands Even Had To Form Some Type Of
Situation From Unity – And As Life When
Discovered At The Soonest Times, We Ask An
Overnight Underground Civic Question From
Where Movement Happens.

To Me– Then As This New Situation Occurs,
Then At Split When This World War Third
Time At The Third Time Arrived – What We
Soon Will Be Safe And Sound Around, Is In
This Life, From Ancient History?

The Only One Rule Made Of Laws If
Fullness To Appear – In Then The States Is
Run By Individuals In Laws – From The
Governmental, President Desk's Orders At This
Time and Place Of the Desk – What Life Then
Is Taken From The President's Chair – Takeoff
Of the United States From The Formations To
An Agreement – Made In USA Dallas, Texas –
That To Mark My Words, "Another World War
Of World War Three!"

This Third Times Of Christ's Life Means –
Alone That World War Three Exists Towards
The Status From A New America, As The Life
From Independent Life Forms Exist and
Endings, Can Happen And Occur – And From
The Jurisprudence And In Divergent Laws
However, The Land We May Hold, In What

Does Exist, No Longer The Laws But Of
Freedoms

I, Can See That The Good And The Sold
Souls From Another Ancient Aged Man, Is
From Who Has, To The Modern Day Man, Of
How An New World Oder Exists, From An
Aged Old Order, Situation And From The
Offers Of Another New Aged Faith Exists Into
How Heaven Appears, And Exists –

This World War Is From However Texans
Win, In The Whole Wide World Over And
Over The Making From Man – From The Texas
Traditions From The Overall Achievers, In the
World War Three

In How To Win Over Allied Forces From
Undergrounds Government Forming of
Intelligence – Toward Protections Over All of
the Global Elite, Thematic Events Of All Life,
In My Plans of the Hidden in Secrets of the
Service From the Spots Around the New World
Order's Empire of Global Elites

To This Winning Of Wars – A Whole Deal
From Antichrist America's National Approach –
From the Plan From The Antichrist Escapism
Philosophy of the National Interest Of The
State Being Annihilated to From A Happening
Life's Coming, An Evil Country, Of Atomic
Bombs, in the Atomic Age of Atomic Bombs.

To Protection, America Is Our Best War!
Idea From American Supportive Interest From
The Free People, As An New Absolute Utopia
of the State I've Existed In And Have Seen, At
What Has Come To Civics, Or Of The Rights
Of Everyone Of The Human Race, As

Liberating Beings, Our US Have Fought In
Wars. It Has, Already Been Days and in It since
One Day, When I've Asked To Seek God And
To See The Antichrist, He Will Nationally
Appear, Togetherness.

All Of The Allied Forces From American
Systems Of Designed Intellectual
Interpretations, And For The Forces Of
England and All Darkness and Good Sides To
Win Over World War Three's Good From True
American People, There Are In Similar Forms
of Protection of the People, of the United States
of America's Government, Alive and Well.

The Past, History, In the New World Order's
Ways – Into Them Approaching From One Life
There Exists Movements From The Justice
Protecting Our System of Body of Warring
Stated Allied Motions, To The World Ahead In
Its Life, Wherein At Life, Therein Happens War

The Governmental Trying From Past Time's
Lifetimes Of American Learning From the
Past's Mistakes, of Israel and Allied Forces, Are
Winning World War Three Of Approach, To
The Destiny Of The People – On The Country
Of America

Places We Go In Life's Wars – Nations and
Democracies, for the World War Three

People That We Meet In This Life – Can
Come From Places As To Where We Go –
From Texas To The World Table – Soldiers
Eating The Blood Of The Lamb – Sacrificial
Rights For The World War Three – Of
Anyone's Lifeblood Made to Serve – Gold
Offers

New World Order Made To Win Over Every
Person - Made In This Life or Into The Live Of
Mine – How Everyone's Gold From World War
Three Planning to Remake Texas – Ideologists
Who Make The World War Happen – When As
None Other Than The Real God's Creation –
The Holy Bibles Made Not Of Hypocrisy, Then
Are Introduced to the World of War a Third
Time In The History's Pages

American New World Order (Sold In Offers)
– To Russian Communist Government – Lead
By "Vladimir Putin: If Lost Life" – A Former
KGB Spy- and a Russian Soldier of Fortune!
USA, World Leaders, Will Enter, Entirely Into;
Wars!, The Killings of an Russian Army, If
Corrupt In The Communist Homeland, Of
Governing Russia?

Vladimir Putin's Scandal – Madman with a
New Communist Manifesto – "New Order" –
Like Adolf Hitler, with his Nazis – Trying to
Lead World War Three With Extremist Scheme
– Is the Bad Guy – Who We Will Fight as the
American Way

All of the World War Leaders Are the Perfect
Soldiers Toward – Their Lives Came From
These Adjacent Sides From Communist and
Republic Style Formations From the One-
World Government, Of One Man

The History As The Same Ad Repetitions
From Two Times of Failed Sold Antichrist's
Aged Golden Offer to the New World's Order
– The News of Everyone Except the New
World Order From America's New Aged
Systematic Trusted Lives, A Deal As Agreed

and Arrived at the Conclusion that the New World Order Was the Denial From Jesus Christ the Lord's – A New Nation Comes From War – After the World Denial of Jesus Christ

In Present Day – Already Happened – The United States Presidents Sold Their Souls To A National Cause – A "New World Order" of the Intelligent Design – From A System of Capitalism To World War Three, of Anti-Hitler Ideology, to Form World Soldiers a Third In The Times With Justice

Leaders (old) Taught All Americans How To Fight – A New World Order, to Form Overnight, After the Precursor of WWII – All USA Soldiers To Introduce An New WW3 – From Methods of Practice and to, Warfare's Costs!

American Leadings In Times From War From How - We Tried From Old World Wars, Three Forms In Victory Over The Antichrist From America – Unknown Takeover The World

Positions of Power From Men Who Ruled The Globe From The Elite Positions Of The Power Held Manifest In The Constitution of the USA

Places of Interests Won Worlds Over From Why Men Fight From War's Glories

White Men's Themed Power Of Democratic Forces From The Allied Government, of Dallas Texans

People In Charge Of American System From Its Design

Presidents (new) Made In A New World
Order America From WWIII!

Chapter 4 –

AND RESPONSE TO

Chapter 4 –

THE ULTIMATE WW3 PLANS OF WAR

Parts from Plans
Whole Introduction
Middle Class Workers

National Leading Causes
Lands over Common Bond's Interest
Countries from Wars
Past Lives' Sold Souls
Present Ages from War
World's Past Times of Deals

Jesus Christ Is In Trinity
God Is In Three Persons
Holy Spirit Is God's Spirit Too

Americans Are the First in War World
World People Are Of Worlds
Plan of Action from Meanings

Buildings for Action
Towers To Command
Hideouts To Construct

Churches Of Worship Of The False God
Synagogue Placed Jewish People

Temples Of Designing Wars
Places In Life As Hurt America
Roman Temple Of Biblical Antichrist
Past Times From Aged Old Wars
Soldiers Fighting For The Cause
Areas Limited To World War
Plans Of Interception

Model America Fights
Club of Rome Secret Life
Parties of Political Deemed Acceptance

SAVED IS CHRIST

Church Is Saved Regardless of Wars

Cities Plan Church's Remodeled Formations

Plans Of War Action
Cities From Hiding Out
United States Is Found In WWIII

Killing Is Deemed As Acceptable
Saving The Soul Is Impossible
Healing The Mind As Good

Nations Form Parties, Overhearing Justice
Democracies Create Philosophy's Endings
Countries Cannot Kill Presidents
Futures   Of   Past's   Construction
Pasts From Denials Of Wars

Present Times Of Country

Times Of Life As Denials
Distances Between You and Me
Path Is From Distances From The War

Light In These Illuminati's Circles
Way End's In The Pyramid of Gaza
Truth Is Wisdom Over Everyone's Time
Antichrist Is Made To Win WW3
America Is His Superpower
USA Won The War From Distances
Beautiful Creations From War's Succeeding Days
Magnificent Beauty Of Lights
Gorgeous America From Antichrist
Paths Of Forgivable Triumph Over Life
Roads From Paving The World's Lives
Streets Form Pictures From The Past Life
Police Cars Pave The Way For The Futures
Ambulance Drivers Are The Coming Home
Fire Truck Protects All Innocent Peoples
     The Sections From My True Ways From
     Knowledge Of Wars

     False Life In The Mind From Man Verses
     Man's Knowledge

Past Lived Knowing
As The Issued Pains
Of Other Life
Forms In The Universe

     Sold Souls To Win Over Jesus Christ From
     The Antichrist

     Bought Life Asking If Jesus Christ Was A
     Savior?

     Freedom as the Life Form of War's

     America As The Solid Objection

     The US Souls Brought To Freedom

Our   USA   Texas   Family   Wynne's

Country Made From Freedom
Land Is Our Property
Property Of American War

FIGHT FOR AMERICAN CAUSE

Rights For The American Public
Liberties And Justices For All
Jesus Christ's Bibles
God Is Three-In-One
The Holy Spirit Lives Within Myself
Give Freedom The Chance To Win
Earn Life As A War Hero
Live Noble Life As Everlasting God
Fights Over Equal Rights Of Its USA Individuals
Wars Won Over Evil Causes
Riots Occur Nationwide In Foreign
Live Lessons On The Power of America
Learn Life And Become Better Than Enemy
Know More From Life And Deaths
Animal Symbols Of Flags, Banners, Signs
Countries Signs From War Animals Representing
Flags Designed To Show Colors Of War
What Life Brings To The Table
How Death Knows Its Limits
Why USA Wins Overall

People Rights As Saved
Souls Saved In Eternity
Lives Earned Of Wars

Reasons Only Why War Wins
Examples From American Wars

Points In America Winning
      WARTIMES OVER AMERICANS

    Battle Born Of New Prepared America

    Fight Its All In The Tables From Presidents

    USA SPIRIT IS IN WHAT WINS
            WAR

    One Nation As Under Our God's Pledge

    United People In War's Common Cause

WORTH IT ALL FOR THE WINS
OF AMERICA

Done Before Its Already Happening
Finished Already The Wars Ending
      STARS REPRESENT FALLEN
              STATES

STRIPES COVER ALL OVER THE
FLAGS

    Flag of USA Risen Americans Tradition

Soldiers to the End of the Worlds
Military Personnel of Government Figures
Air Forces Made In the Image of War
Guards In The Entrances Of Another World
Weapons In Wars Win Over Unjust Countries
Machines of War Designed To Kill Enemies
    Peace Plans Came From The USA One-
World Government

War's Plot to End the World of the Antichrist

World At War From Fighting Old Wars

INTELLECT KNOWN OVER ALL OF THE USA

Mind Thoughts Occur From National's Identity

Imagination Does Do Right Things To Our USA

Hideouts To Keep People Safe
Base Camps Not Like Nazi Germany
Planning Spots Like Hitler's Eagle's Nest
The USA Won Already
NWO As America Won

My Life Is Example

Secrets of the USA
Hidden Knowledge Places

Guarded Places of Secret Life

War Bombs
Weapons of Destruction
Atomic Age

Annihilation of USA
Destruction of Our Lands

Dead USA From War

Underground Books
Hidden Agendas
Plots to Destruction

Whole World At War   (WWIII)
The Worlds At War (US)

The Wars of the World (Worldwide)

Freedom Idealized (USA)
Democracy Improved (USA)
Lands Free And Protected (World)

The Soldiers Fighting
The Machines
The Men

Fight For Freedom
Guard the Homeland
Make   Safe   The   USA

No Terrorism
Anti-Extremists
Laws Against Aliens

Antichrist America
Biblical "666"
One Man

Starts World War 3
Misleads World To War
Leads America Astray

SATAN
FOUR CORNERS OF EARTH
KILLS OFF EVERY NATION

Beast

"Revelations"
Enemy

Myself
Riley Miller
World Leader

Charmer
Gentleman
Leader

One Person
Two Leaders
Free & Sold

One Soldier's
Mind Control
Worships The Beast

The Story of War
The Plot Of WW3
The World War Third Time

The Third World War
The Third Time War
A "USA" World War

THE SECRET WAR

President   of   USA
The One Man

Stolen War's Office
Future War's Office
Past War Office

Made Money
Mad Expense
Huge Spending

Atomism of Spending Dollars
Expenses For Plans
War Money Plots

Laws Of Anarchy
No Protected Lands
Rights Of Life

Doom As Destiny
Antichristian Plans
Anti-American Plot Man's

FREEING OF THE MIND

Slavery   Laws   of   USA
Anti-Rights (As Foreigners)

Soldier Protecting Homes
Foreign Laws
American Laws

Peopled Culture
Peopled Laws
Human's Rights

People are People
Rights are Rights
Laws are Laws

Homeland As Security

Laws Protecting Lives
Pro-Peopled For Laws

Free War's Land
Pro-action Wars
Free And Easy Laws

The USA War After WWII
The American War
USA War's End

Laws of War
Freedom of the Country
End of America

Storage of Food
War's Resource
Humanity's Natural Foods

Supplies to Help Maintain Desire
Food To Feed The Mouths
Resources of Natural Substance

New Order Is Old Plan Of WWII
New Age In Current Time Is Good
World Order Can Create WWIII
           FOREIGN PROTECTION FOR USA
                   PEOPLE

       Homeland Guard Represents Free Americans

       America Is War From The Ends Of The
Earth

       Antichristian America Fights Armies In WWIII
       Anti-humanistic Laws Keep Sacred The US
Mind

Anti-America Should Not Be Right
Find Plots Of Money, Gold, and Soldiers
Design For War's Plans and Plots Thicken
Humanity's Third End of the World We Live In
The Will To Power Enters The Picture of
Antichrist

The Mind of Destruction Is Enemy Plot To
End Christ

The Heart of Design Carries Home Pictures
of Madness

Beauty of Vision Of War From Times Spent
are Valued

Boldest Plan of Free World, Is Designed By
Antichrist

Magnificent Fall of the USA Is Made To Be
Happening

The Hated Leaders Plot to End Good In Evil
Minded Laws

The Foreign Places Protected By America Is
For WWIII

The USA Wins Easily By Antichrist, And
Force of Its Will

One Man To Hell And Then World War
Three Is the Devil

Leadership In The Formation of Followers
Populate the Lands

Follow USA Is In This War, Idea and
State,   From   Annihilation

Spots of Plots Design the War Machines, Of Our Nation's Arms

Plans for USA To Win, Made Possible, By The Aristocratic Elite

The USA War, Spreading and Constructing, the Image of A Man

Holy Church's Decisions, Is In The Bible, From God's Elitists

Masses, Help Feed, Clothe, and Shelter, the Misfortunate

AMERICA'S ONE MAN IS THE ANTICHRIST

States of Anarchy of the World's Diseased, Come Cured

Protection of War Is From America's Decision, To Die

Safety On Warring States Is The Savior of the World Duty

Plotting Of Mass Destructions, Can and Will, Plot To Win

Christ's Deformation, From His Crucifixion, Leads the World

Destruction and the Demolishment, of the Government, Is Untrue

Free Citizenship To American's Nationalism, Being Approved

World Freedom, Spreads America's Message

Democracy's Laws, Enforced And Reinforced, Do Never Exist

The USA Wins, In Freedom of the People, Who Died For A Cause

The American Wins World War 3, Forging a Path, To End Creation

The Entire US Won, And All Lost, To the World Order

The Wins of WWIII Of One Man Land From Leaderships, Arrive From USA Homeland

Wins Evil No Longer, Defeated By the Good

Good World, Carries Home All War, Freedom Fighters

Evil Wars, Against the Good of Peace, Construct Anarchy

Freeing Win, The Human Valued Cost, To The Valued, Saved Model

War Song's, Decreeing Method, Risen to USA Top Window Viewed, Over All

Desires, Around the Circled Man of Sin, Can Be Carried On, Too Long, For Win

Meanings, The Antichrist Makes, Is Valueless

My Country, Is The Song, Repeated, As If It Was WW2 Unto WW3

Americanism Is The Song, That Fights All USA Wins, Of Other Countries

Homelands of America, Then In Fighting
From Our Freedom, Wins By Its Choices

Targeted Enemy Awareness, Counts Up Bid,
Until the Antichrist Comes, To Earth

War Time, In Losing Countries, Means That
Supplies and Goods, Are Valued As The Least

World Good, And My Humanity, Is Not
Overvalued, In World War Three, In Beginnings

Man of Lies, Who Cheats, Destroys, Kills,
The Status Quo, of America In The End

Deceiver Means No Good, Who Denies
Works, And Satan As Good, Deceives All

Satan's Person Is In WWIII, Who Is One
Voice, One Mind, And One Person (A.C.)!

Biblical and Churched Peopled Masses, Are
Saved From Sins, Who Lose By War

Christ's Following, of His Body, Replaced By
The Messes, The Olden Past Has Made

Followers of the New World Order, Are
Counted, In The Act and Deed, For The USA

One Person, Can Win World War Three, By
Believing In God, And Going To Church

Triple-Six, Is The Mark of the Man, From
Envisioned, Parts of the World, He Controls

Man of USA's Intelligence, Made The Man
Of Lies, Into A Condemnable Unity Of All

Know Enemy And Face Of Nation, Arguing
Over Lands, and Skies, In the Wrong Way

One World of the USA, In One Fact, Is That
The American Nation Is Protected, From Hurt

Triumph USA, Over The Laws, Of The
Land, Keep Out Foreigners, From Open
Entering

Fears To the World, Came From Phobia, Of
the World, That It Is, Lead By Evil Makings

Safety Of Our People, In Lands of God's
Freedom, Except the Enemies, Of Communism

Person, As The Americans, In This Life, Has
Been One Man, From Ruling the World War

Philosophy Is The Act, and Deed, and Mark,
of an American, When He Thinks Alone

Killing Is As Certain, The Privilege From War
Beholds, Accepting the Wrong Way, Of An
Man

Justice, Is the Position of the Laws, Into the
War

Man's War Came True, And Lost and Won,
Everywhere In The Warring World

Home Win Are Family and Friends, Winning
A War Alive As Ourselves, In Victory

Lands of Freedom Are Designated, As Roles,
Citizens Play, To Enter Into The USA

Heart Is Made, And Controlled, By The
Wars, Until It Is Freed, Of The Victory Wins

Enemy Of the World, Is Any Anti-US Victim
or Oppressor, Winning By Desire To Lose

Killings Acted Out, In The Measured Worth
of a Person, In Life Founded From Our Lands,
Can See Heaven, From National Duties

National Land, Is Our Forefather's Country,
That We Protect, As Your And My, Land

American Land, As Of Soil, Could Be As The
War Dictates, That What Is Won, Is Won

USA Soil, Agreed With By The Government,
As The Person Directed, Are Agreeable Won

Conferences in The Life From Businessmen,
Could Hurt And Harm, Any Individual, In War

Meetings, Are For Meetings, Wherein People,
From All Over The World, Are Safety First

Rooms, Of Our Design, Are There To Help
Protect, All Laws Of Our Nation, Under God

In Secrets, Of the American Values System,
Into the Motion and Duties, Of Our Great
Land, We Are Innocent

For Production of American Values, The
Trusted Side Always Wins, In Good Ways

Talks, From the Old, And the New, Can
Enter Into Thoughts, In Appearing Doubts

Enter, To Heaven, and Leave To Hell, If You
Want To Play, War Games, With Its USA

Leave the Door to War, As an Adventure
Open, To the Public of the American Ways,
Win's, The Minded Games, Of American
Soldiers!

The USA's Religion, and in the Christian
Church, Peace and Good Things, Bring One
Closer To God, In the Church

Decides of the Fallen Empire, of Ancient
Rome, There Were Choices, Of War That Made
Them Fall

Fights Over Disputed Lands, Are Chosen
From USA, Property Of Our Mind's Eye, All
As Protected

Intelligence Is Thought Of, Well-off In The
United States of America's Presidency,
Especially By Us – All! X

Open Wars Meant Abolition Of All Human Rights
Best Minds Works For Philosophy
Closed Minds, Are Ignorance
Selections, Of The Property Of The "USA's,"
How Minds Control The World

Peaceful, Communities Entrance, Into the
World Of The Idea, Of Life

Community, As The People Involved, Harm
and Hurt, The Democracy, Of The USA

Battles Are Life's, Great Choices
Births, Happen When War
Death, Is Alive, In God

Generals, Are The Actors, From Another
War's Times

Presidents, Are Leaders, Of The Chosen
Faith, In The USA

War Leaders, Believed In Their Country, To
Fight Enemy

Planner, War
Decider, Fates
Plotter, Destiny

    Americans Who Win
    One War Has All Americans
    Citizens Are The Good People

Church, Decides
Chapel, Surround The Soul
Bases, Control Points of Duty

    NEW, BEGIN WORLD WAR THREE

    Old,   Repeat   World   War   Two
Secret, Stolen Lives of WWIII

New American People, Actions Are Great
Old Allied Forces Put Together Lives
New American Forces, Won Together
    I WIN, OVER EVIL

    Peopled Win, Over American Nation

    American's Wins, Over Slavery

United States of America Wins All Wars
Foreign Land of Killing at the USA
Lands Won, Protect the American Public
Enemy, Of The Foreign Lands, Is Communist
    New Order, Is Movement of WWII,
Communism Party

    Communism, A Gathered Idea That Can Not
Work, And Is Evil

Sold, Government of One World

Bought, The Presidential Candidates
Fought, In the War Yesterday
Philosophy, The Movement of Greatest Thinkers

New Aged Order, Succeeds
Books, Tried and True, From Myself
Freedoms, Democratic Idols
Callings, God's Answer
Orders, Are All Good

Laws, Determined
Bylaws, Decided
Legal, Courts

Courts, Justice
Caste Laws, Heredity
Ranks, Followed

System, Government
Followings, USA
Democracy, Popularity of Presidents

Illuminated Ones, War's Illuminati
Idea, Knowledgeable
Christ, God

Army, Soldiers
Wins, War
Soul, Sellable

Legal, Represented
Illegal, Unintelligent
Record, Documented

Peace, USA
War, Foreign

I,   **Me**

Sold, New World Order
Bought, WW Plans
Purchased, Three Orders

Poor, Lowly
New, Founded
Family, True Life

Budgeting, Money
Fees, Collections
Signatures, Identity

President (USA), The Whole New World's King
Final Judgments, The Last Ends of All Worlds
World War Ending, Judgment's Day Is Here Soon
Life, Lived At America's Deaths
Deaths, Death from Life Is Not Alive
Cost, Counted In Days 'Till WWIII
Pen, In Hand To Sign Laws
Hand, Cursive
Agreement's, Signature

Intellect, Mind
Mind, Thoughts
Attitude, Christian

Evangelist, Pastor
War, Worldly
Backer, Supportive

Finance, Dollars
Money, Financial
Ending, Statements

Alliance, Old Wars
World War, Third Time
Agreements, Settled Issue

Killing Ceases, World Peace
Friend Agreements, Negotiations
Superpowers, War Machines
Hot, Burnt
Cold, Frozen
Lukewarm, Hearts

World, United States
War, Enemies
Third, Numbered

Past, Old
Now, Immediate
Future, Light

Call, Beckon
Summon, Cometh
Believed, Knowledge

Triple, Deaths
World, Hated
War, Sought

Everyone, All
Everything, Itself
Everywhere, Overall

President, Elections
Official, Profile
War, Evil

Chair, Leader
Office, Highest
Leader, Powerful

Time, Moments
Chair, Supportive
Presidents, Chiefs

Deal, Agreements
Man, Person
Staff, Collective

Oilmen, Richest
Money, Making
Costs, Spent

Man,
Deed, Works

Alive

Price, World

Sold, Itself
Pen, Signature
Paper, Medium

Forgive, Sorry
Press, Followings
Media, Coverage

Coverage, Overlord
Public, President
Person, Humanity

More, Above
Less, Lowly
All, Itself

Life, Living
Learn, Deciding
Brains, Minding

Pen, Agreements
Paper, Valuable
Golden, Sought

Weights, Strongly
Influence, Design
Decision, Remarkable

Hot, Rooms
Cold, Outside
Middle, Pathways

Missile, Atomic
Bomb, Nuclear
Annihilation, Extinction

More, Above
Less, Lowly
Monetary, Collectives

Start, Beginning
Finish, Ending
Middle, Undecided

Home Land
Legendary – Lives of One Man
Pay X-Generation Money

Fares At War's Ending
Benjamin's Dollar, Signed
Money,

Ben
Jeff
Sally

America
People
Trust

Deal
Decide
Pensions

Dollar
Dead
Presidents

Sign
Contract
Signature

Not
Yes
Handshake

Deal
Soldiers
Anybody

War
Peaces
Agreements

Person
Guard
Ideas

Power
Plans
Bombs

Rights
Law
Order

Victory
Reach
Succeed

Troubles
Ending
Battle

All
Over
Destruction

USA
Homeland

Outreaching

Cold
Desires
Soldiers

Noteworthy
Surprised
Legends

A.C.

War
Death

Lasting
Friends
Country

Religion
Laws
Soil

Final
United States
War

World Of The Third War
Globe Is Intact With Enemies
Whole Map Of America

Succeed In Armies
Knowing US Constitution
People Are Saved

Living In Texas, For Family
Dying For Nation, Armies
Learning The Methods Of War

Lifelong War Parties
Jews Of The Torah
Biblical Countries

    4 Corners Of The Earth
    Satan Is The Deceiver
    American War In Texas

Whatever
Brought
Warring

Relived
Won
WW2

Third
America
Final

Three
Start
Finish

Evil
Good
Neutral

Top
Bottom
Middle

Lead
Follow
God

Win
Lose
Failure

Promote
Savings
Followings

Peaceful
Sold
Philosophy

Old Aged
New Aged
Present Ages

Sold
Idea
Teach

Fails
Loses
Wins

Billionaire
Backers
Financial

Produce
Find
Go Forth

See
Learn
Hear

War
Deaths
Killing

Go

Forth

Preside

Look
Know
Run

Seek
Find
Yield

Products
Flow
Rankings

Top
Spot
God

Hate
Life

Examine

Top
Spot
Known

Resources
Money
Billionaires

RAW

Material
Resource

China
Russia
Germany

Meaning
Leader
Rules

Highest
Life
Tops

Lesson
Learning
Products

Wars
Godly Man
Army

Golden
Money
Supply

Bank
Hideaway
Safety

Find
People
Churched

Little
Big
Wars

Bad
Evil
Good

New
Order
World

Light
Caves
Outside

WORLD

War
Three

Want
Knowing
Plots

Evil
Wicked
Vile

Raw
Element
Materials

Human
Color
Races

Life

Deed
Rights

Story
Tales
Victims

Wrong
Right
Middle

Wealth
Money
Classes

World
Wars
Third

I
NOA
AIC

One
Man
War

Sold
Buys
World

Cured
Disease
Schizophrenia

High
Low
Middle

Class
Society
Culture

Fort
Bunker
Door

Today
World
Three

News
Medias
Press

Private
Secretive
Hides

Modern
New
Present

Called
Summoned
Life

     Summoned
   Believed

Known

First
Second
Third

President
First
Beginning

World
Spread
Omniscient

Planning
Reading
Finality

Plots
Plans
Product

Universes
Little
Highest

New World Order – American
Old World Order – British
World Orders In Both – Old And New Allied Parts

Around
Planned
Age

Knowledge
Christianity
Order

Pen
Paper
Purchases

Seek
Worldly
Wonders

Home
Returned
Front

Reach
Total
Outside

World
Wide
War

Stop
Height
Place

Work
Action
Knew

Stops
Ceased
Exiled

Oldness
New
Ordered

Buying
Selling
Finance

Buy
Sold
Knowledge

Brains
Banned
Police

Kills
Deals
Society

News
Old
Sellable

Hot
Cold
Newness

Buying
Powers
Limited

Intellect
Powers
Limited

Intellect
Powering
Foretold

Sold
Buying
Finality

Sanity Impossible To Handle
Insanity Mind Control Microchips
Mediums Thoughts In Channels
Control Mind Of The Person
Mind Forced To Be Alike All
Number Marked On All Foreheads

Three Sixes Control Mind As Number

Forehead Marked 3-6's Transparently

Wrist Labeled Triple-Six Invisibility

Beast's Menaced Mind Is Animalistic
Antichrist's Identity Is Insanity
Satanic USA Madmen

I   –   America's   Self
NOA – New Order of the Ages, Readable
Books
NO   –   New   Order,   Hitler's

New – Age Of War
Age – Old Times
Ordered – Life and Times

Sold - Soul
Souls - Deceived
Desires – For Knowledge of the Apple

Big
Small
Medium

Noted
Pensions
War

Bank
Profits
Spent

Fortitude
President
World

Spending
Earnings
Allowances

Spent
Dollars
Sense

Plans
Peace
Wars

Top
Hideouts
Controls

Peace
War
Plotting

Spots
Hideaways
Secret Spots

Old
New
Camp

Wealth
Abundance
Life

Times
New
Olden

Days
Dates
Hours

Names
Position
Success

Gold
Silver
Bronze

Ends
Spending
Begin

Going
Out
Places

Militaries
Soldiers
Armies

Hate
Pride
Goings

Lens
Sight
Seeing

Philosophy
Perspective
Viewpoints

Doubts
Faithful
Reliant

Friend
Foe
Accomplice

Polices
Enemy
Crimes

Poorest
Richest
Millionaires

Power
Ability
Rights

Power
Nothingness
True

Sellable
Bought
New World Order

Matters
Truest
Strength

Highest
Most
Offices

Strongest
World
Wars

Nothing
Sent
Gradual

Peaces
World
War

Offices
Government
I

One-World Government

Fed

CIA

Five Most Powerful Men
Philosophy From Wars
New Order Of The Ages

New Order
Enemy
Communists

Party
Vladimir Putin
Political Leader

Academics
Learning
History

Pasts
Wars
Wins

Old
Offices
Repeated Officials

Identical
World Wars
Three of Them

State
Higher Power
Officials

Highest

Politics
Highest Point's

World War
Three
Vladimir Putin

Presidents
Past Offices
War's Politics

Russia
China
			Anti-USA

Myself
My Office
President

Cold
Hot
Measures

Love
Hated
Relations

Find
Lost
Leading

Leads
Leading
War

Officials
Pasts
Presidents

Lovers
Haters
Doers

Hurt
Help
Goodness

One Cause
USA
One Man

Foundations
Nationality
Solid Rights

Research
Finding
Discovery

     USA
  WWIII
    I

Books
Discussions
Plans

Introduction
Plan
War

Democracy
Socialism
Communism

Three-Numbered Sixes
The Mark On The Forehead
The Method Of Control

Mind and Body
Thoughts and Intellect
The Triple-Six

Anti
Against
Opposing

Cause
Man
Humanity

Strongest
Powerful
Greatest

Test
Caused
Triumphed

      Won
   All

    Yesterday

Perfect Leader
Angry Man

Man of Reasons

Treasons
Faces (Many)
Identity

Treasured
Sought After
Known Evil

Antichrist
America
Person

3-6's
Animal
Beast

Armageddon
End Times
Apocalypse

End of the World
Numbered
Days

Counted
Lives
People

Games
Lives
Followers

All
Nations

Followers

Nations
World
Antichrist

USA
Everyone

Blindly

Few
Many
Forced

Smartest
Dumb
Realized

Works
Counted
Rewarded

Forgiveness

Sorry
Innocent

ID

Mad
Sorry

Identity
Bar-Coded
Mind

Controlled
Readings
Forceful

Brain
Forehead
Mind

Controlled
Purchased
Slavery

Triple-Six
Thoughts
Forced

One
Person
"Man"

Bible
Antichrist
"666"

Hell
Afterlife
Doomsday

Entrance
Eternal
"Satan"

Real
Official
Identity

Found-Out!
Realized
Defrauded

DECODED

World   War   III
Antichrist

One Man
America
        USA

History
Living
Final Days

Judgment Day
Jesus On White Horse
Ending of Earth

Bad
Evil
Hell

God
Right
Heaven

        USA
Riley Miller

Identity

Righteous
Heavenly
Angels

Rebellion
Satan
Heaven

Fought
Won
Fell

War
World
Three

Plus
Minus
Middle

Ours
Land
Everyone's

Free
Laws
Lands

Song
Dance
Rhythm

War
Treatises
Appointing

Minds
Body
Humanity

Personality
Classes
Hierarchy

The End
The Antichrist
The Apocalypse

WWIII
WWII
WWI

Happy
Flourishing
Better

Wins
Victory
Success

Black
White
Clearest

Forehead
Arm
Hand

666
One Man

Beast

Nothing
Clearness
Void

Darkness
Intelligence
Wonder

Light
Cave
Chains

No
Yes
Definite

Either
Or
Singular

Win
Lose
Void

       Know
   Think

    Action

Tanks
Aircrafts
Boats

Jets

Pilots
Sailors

War
Declare
World

    AC

        USA
  All

One
Nation
War

One
World
War

Repeat
3rd
War

Private
Public
Information

Economic
Government
People

Constitution
Bill of Rights
Emancipation Proclamation

Treatise
Documents
Handshakes

Church
Political
Speakers

Rules
Serves
Democracies

Worldwide
Wartimes
Three

President
Staff
Vice-President

Officials
Dignitaries
Magnates

Importance
Officially
Beneficial

Pro
Positive
Support

Life
Success
Gaining

Wars
Battles
Fights

Fright
Fears
Courage

Made
Decided
Attempt

"Pro"
"Con"
Declined

Jointly
Chiefs
Staff

Meeting
Gather
Socialite

Matters
Choices
Decisions

Walk
Fly
Ride

Strongest
Mind

IQ

Man
Person
Numbered

Decided
Chosen
Marked

Ordered
Newness
Worldly

I
WWIII
Light

Idea
Forehead
Number

Idol
Bible
Evil

Man
One
All

Evil
Good
Mark

Evil
Goodness
Liberty

Causes
Effects
Celebrated

Wars
Winning
Sides

Killing
Vision
Innocent

Murdered
Shot
Overpowered

Life
Persons
Allegiance

I
WWIII
AIC

Books

Manuals
Textbooks

Strongest

Smartest
Smarter

America
Russia
China

Survival
Contestant
Winner

Biblical
Antichrist
America

USA
Wins

Challenges

Presumption
Guessed
Factoid

USA
Wins

WWIII

Americans
WWIII's
Kills

Place
Date

Time

America
End Times
At Hand, The Hour Is

Evolution
Warfare
Survivors

Weakest
Strongest
Powerfulness

Kings
Nobility
President's

Soldiers
Fighting
Constructions

Remade
Pre-chosen
Fittest

Dallas
Santa Fe
Oxford

Texas
New Mexico's
England

Street
School

Independent

Smarts
Skills
Ability

Testing
Scoring
Learning

Perhaps
Maybe
Decidedly

Skillfully
Planning's
Masterful

Deadly
Alive
Living

Killed
Lifeless
Shot

Murdered
Killed
Assassinated

Laws
Rules
Legalities

Known
Popular

Famous

Readable
Plausibly
Scorings

Report
Documents
Treatise

Taken
Seized
Victorious

Class
Status
Report's

Social
Economic
Philanthropy

Hired
Recruited
Support

Earth
Planet
World

Decreed
Pronounced
Determined

Trains
Cars

Planes

Badness
Good
Reliable

Occupying
Seizing
Takeover

Terrain
Nature
Territory

Pride
Satisfaction
Agreeing

Homes
Offices
Workplace

Schools
Hospitals
Prisons

Lands
Freedoms
Democracy

Idealism
Fictional
Imagination

Party
Republican

Each

Party
Political
Past

Newness
Recruited
Followings

Ability
Purchase
Directedness

Belief
Life
Change

Old
New
War

Sold
Deformed
Tarnished

Lives
Hearts
Souls

Home
Work
Schooling

Three
Time-Span

Knowledge

Sided
Party
Slummed

Soldiers
Military
Fighters

Recipe
Information
Selections

Articles
News
Papers

Popularity
Gossip
Slander

Local
Distance
Nearby

Tops
High
Peak

Lands
Freedom
Fought

Smarts
Perfect

Skill

Targets
Groups
Grounds

Philosophy
Debate
Questions

Soldier
Kill
Save

Man
Antichristian
Human

Alive
Dead
Chosen

New World Order
Alliances
Old World Order

Banners
America's
Ownership

Saintly
Sinner
Freeing

Water
Food

Clothing

Adventure
Protective
Defending

Psyche
Atlas
Crazy

In Wars
Dialectical
Deranged

Promoting
Killings
Badges

Love
Neighbor
Peaceful

Attitude
Aggressive
Respect

Bodies
Training
Welfare

Pastors
Sermon
Death

Medals
Brave

Courage

Intelligence
Most
War-Times

Heroism
Activeness
Ranks

Plotting Points
Control Worlds
Decide Plans

Amazing
Structures
Capability

WINNERS

USA
Greatest

Duties
Saved
Lives

Great War
Unified
America

Glorified
Attributed
Adventures

Three Six's
One Person (Man)
Beware a Man

Duty
Active
Committed

Called
Service
Manhood

Holocaust
Relived
WW2 Of WW3

Predictions
Destruction
Humankinds

Visionary
Antichrist's
Following

Every Nation
The Triple-six
All Of Everyone

Warring
People
Following

The Antichrist
The Three Sixes
Mark On Forehead

Third World War
Freedom
American's A.C.

Win   The   USA
Over All The World

America Sole Nation

Everyone Following
Everything Controlled
Everybody Marked

USA President Obama
Watches Carefully
Role As Entire US

Killings Acts
Brotherhood Fighting
Soldiers Dying Forever

Washington, D.C.
Control Person's Desk
Presidential Control Point

LOVE THY NEIGHBOR

Birthed   USA
Plan of Antichrist

Bombs Foreign Land
Attack Anti-American
Foreign Annihilation

USA'S WHOLE WORLD

<pre>
Reconstruct   USA
USA Wins Over All
</pre>

The Club of Rome
The Societies of Places (USA)
<pre>
        The   War   Recruiting   USA
</pre>

<pre>
War

        Easy
Hard
</pre>

Demands
Constructing
Buildings

Natures
Man
Animals

Rights
Places
Interest

Decisions
Leaders
Presidents

<pre>
        USA
Worlds
</pre>

War

Warring
Level
Wins

Today
Now
This Moment

Wherein
Whatever
Wherever

  Why   Not?
 Reasons

  Causes

Wartimes
War Spots
War Places

Duty
Plans
Calling

  Duty
 Place

  Things

Followings
Duties
Positions

Persons

Protect
Planet

Heard
Times
Productions

Times
Proclamations
Around World

News
Callings
Built

Persons
Duty
Called

AMERICANS

Native
Productions

USA

World War Three
Playing Fields
USA Citizens

Perchance
Directions
Aims

Spots
Protection
Hearsay

Gathering
Plans
Citizen

Build
Freedom
Plans

Democracy
Party
Republicans

Party
Followings
Reasons

Clubs
Societies
Memberships

Fellowships
Research
Willing

New Age World
The Order
New World Order

Persons
Places
Things

Events
Persons
Places

Chapter 5 –
The World I Made

        Hard Times   American Wars
        Useful Things   Society At Large
Philosophy Of War
States of USA   Places In World
Direction of War
        Foreign Lands   Dire Needs of USA
        Places of Plot
        United States   Foreign Nations
Demand of Needs
Far Away Lands   Up-Close America
Places
United States   Russians
Foreigners
China   Germany
Localities
Allied Forces   United States of America

USA WAR!

Third World War
Destined Into World
Will Come In Time – Due
USA Will Win Everything

Antichrist America!
To End The World – In War
World To Come – USA Victory
Prophesy In Bibles – End Times

APOCALYPSE – WWIII

World of Fear In America
Will Wipe Out Everything
Comes When America Ends

WORLD WAR PLOTS!

Construction of a New America
Rebuilding of Roman Temple

USA'S WARS!

Supply and Demand For Goods
Resources of Needed Materials
Energy From Resources In USA!
Top Soldiers & Armies Brought To!

USA'S PEACES

The Generals and Presidents Protect USA
The Men at War At Home Seek Good
The Supplies Are For War and Peace
The Peace of America Is At Home

AMERICAN PRESIDENT

THE ELECTED PRESIDENT IS FOR WWIII

THE VOTE FOR OFFICE MAKES HIM ELECT!

WAR FOR HIM, WORKED FOR GOOD

World War Three, Is Inevitable.

THE WAR EFFECTIVE

USA Is Homeland
Foreign Is Unprotected
Free Lands Are Good

THE PEACE EFFECTED

Love is a Common Virtue.
Peace is not at all, of wars.
World Peace, is Impossible.

THE MAN IN USA

We Make Our Own Choices.
At War, We Come Around.
The Man Is War-Based.

THE HOME WAR

The USA Is Protected!

No One, Can Destroy It!
America, Is Made To Be, Of Mine!

THE MIND OF AMERICA

Intellect
Mind
Imagination

INSPIRATION

Success
Life

ALL THREE

USA Wars
USA Peace
World War III
Inspired Intellect
Freedom of Minds
The Reason Of Life As Too Much!

MY LIFE

I, have habits. I, want to live, WW3.
I am depressed. I, do not love, life.
I have a reason. I am only a person.

WW3!

Soldiers
Payments
Satisfy
Home Front

War's A Nil
Impossible

Nothing
Something
Any Wars
No
Yes
Every War

Nations
Armies
World
War
Peaceful
Studied

Not
True
Biased
Fulfilled
Promising
Planning

Intellect
Machine
Superpower
Planning
Ideology
Americans

America
World
Third War
American

Gentile
Believers

WARS WORLD WON

Pasts
Now
Kings
Won
Lost
Wartimes

Futures
Now Is How
President
Today
Purchases
Losses

Old   USA
Kingdoms

USA Won
Emergency
Estranged
Topicality

New
Free
Won
Americans
Today
Alive
Fortune
Dealing
Empires

War's Won
Alliances
Newspapers
Pastimes
Present
Changed

The All-About America!
How America Wins WWIII!

Learning lessons, on killing.
Knowing America is innocent.
Trying hard, to know blamed.
To forgive, for tragedy.
To see the USA, in better ways.
Mistakes, are made to remake us.

WHY RILEY MILLER LOSES WWIII!

The Lost.
The Confused.
The Damned.
The Blamed.
War Calling.
War's Enemy.
WWIII Aliens.
World War Loser!

LOSE OR WIN?

Lost America, Means Nothing To Me.

Won America is, my life as good.

"USA'S WW3"

Feel Better.
Know Enemy.
Inspire Friends.
Counsel Brothers.
Win All Over.
Trusts In Oneself.
Treat People Well.
Seek First Good.
Correct No One.
Be a Happy Person!
Guard Your Mind!

AN AMERICAN LIFE!

Riley Miller's World View
Future President of USA
9-11's Deal
World Trade Center
Al Qaeda
Osama Bin Laden
Saddam Hussein
Terrorist Operations
Iraq and Iran War
Baghdad
ISIS Terrorist Group

Why, do we go to WW3?
The American Antichrist

HOW DOES AMERICAN WIN?

Following The Antichrist To War

What is WWIII?
The Apocalypse of Armageddon
How is WW3 Fought?
Weapons of Mass Destruction of USA
Who Wins WW3?
America Wins

WHY IS IT WW3?

The New World Order's Ending!

What does Christ do?
Rider on the White Horse

HOW WW3 IS EVERYDAY?

Tomorrow
Everyone
Sundays
Everything
Everyday's
Each Day
All Days
New Days
Today
Living

WW3 IS EXTINCT!

Failure
Lost
Tries
Losses
Understanding

Damnation
Knowledge
Damned
Intelligent
Hell
Loss Days
Satan
Good Days
Hellishness
Peace

LIFE AND LIFE'S!

Pen
Hand
Sword
Side
Life
Deaths
Under
Armor
Pen
Side
Nail
Foot
Eyeballs
Contact Lenses
Forehead
Hat Brim
Head
Cowboy Hat

DEATH AND DEALS!

Sword
Sheath
Shot
Gun
Wound
Chest
Knife
Wastes

WORLD WAR THREE!

Expense
World Wars
Spending
Learning
Funding
Supportive
Lending
Participant
Sharing
Mutuality
Giving
Lending

(How Money Is Plan)

THE USA'S MONEY!

Wealth of people in WW3
Poorest of those for WW3
Richest of loaners of WWIII
Paid highest of loot for WWIII
Surplus of money in WWIII
Lowest possible in WWIII

High earned dollar valued
Big expenses paid back to
No money earned for value
Giving money to World War

MONEY MEANT NO WARS!

Richest Due to WW3
Least for WW3 In Support
Support through Loans to WW3
Highest Monetary Involved WW3
Most Support for WW3!
No Support from These People
Supported by Giving to Wars
No Show, No Dough in Wars
By Giving then Big Receiving

BIG-TOP FROM WW3'S WAR!

Highest
Entertainment
Payments

Royalty
Payments
Dollars

Checks
Bill
Dollar

BIG

Texas

USA

Pens
Signs
Signature

A SEALED PLAN – WWIII'S USA!

Payments
Banks
Work
Spending
Cash
Accumulated Money
Big Earnings
Riches
Surplus
Money
Cash
Wealth
Banks
Fed
Office

THE LIVES BEFORE WAR!!

Illuminati
Secret Plans
Hidden Agenda
Brotherhoods
Society
Groupings
Movements
Sealed Size
Measured

Republican
Democrat
Conservative
Predetermined
Ready
Sold

THE GROUPS MOVEMENTS TO WW3

Secret
Public
Numerous
Heaven
American
Christian
Growing
Numbering
Larger
Books
Conspiracy
Theory
Mind
Clues
Sad

THE GROWING MOVEMENTS TO WW3!

Atomic
Nuclear
Biological
Racism
Anti-American
Selectivity

Foreign
Enemy
Holocaust
Bombs
Solders
USA Leads
One Man
One Country
One Enemy

WW3 – PLANS TO TAKEOVER
ALL

Selective
Characters
Holy Bible
Global
Movements
Strength
Time
Life
Human
Evil
Good
Will
Power
Enemy
Love
Strive
Hardest
Anger
Big
Sizable
Grows
Spreads
Catches-On

Returns
Every
All
Tripled
Size
Height
Weight
Pro
Con
Null
Force
Power
Enemy
Home
Family
Sacred
Large
Big
Giant
Grows
Forward
Omniscience
End
Talking
Thinking
Dumb
Smart
Mighty

WHEN WW3 BEGINS, WHAT'S?

Communications
Talking
Speaking
All Over

Every Corner
Each Side
Fast
Slowest
Beginnings
Starts
First
New
Fear
Love
Purpose
Shock
Killing
Hatred
Ability
Happy
Smiles
Impacting
Television
Friend
Sides
Choices
Willing
Knowledge
Commentary
Destruction
Frontal
Measured
Sizing
Judgment
Party
Related
Relativity
Evolution
Choices
Easiness

Frown
A-Bomb
Holocaust
Ends
Armageddon
"Hitler Man
Madman Leading
Questionable Life

WORLD WAR III – SPREADING OVER ALREADY!

Soon
Afterwards
Deaths
Camps
Bases
Hidden Spots
Designated
Area
Designed
Walls
Assassins
Miller, Riley
Words
Picture
Internet
Social
Professional
Academic
Towns
Country
Democracy
Lives
Death

Talking
Roads
Bridges
Streets
Captured
Convict
Imprisoned
Life
Beings
Existing
Paths
Roads
Traveled
Peace
War
Already
Secret
Hidden
Unknown
Private
Rooms
House
Demonstrations
Christianity
Churched
Schedule
Events
Christians
Programs
Systems
Confinement
Education
Masses
Idealist
Fast
All

Limits
Story
Tales
Plots
Main
Big
Middle
Front
Lined
Proud
Business
Commerce
Gaining
Law
Order
NOA!
Song
Battle
Sing
Protect
Heard
Dear
Pro-Life
Guards
Cursed
Thrones
Crowned
Castles
Visionary
Product
Illuminated Ones
Weeds
Sicken
Weaken

NOA Or NWO – WWIII "OK"!

NOA

Age Movement
Same
Firstly
Last
3 Letters
King Making
New World Order
"NWO'S King"
NOA
New Order of the Ages
Novus Ordo Seclorum
N.W.O.
Latin
Tree
Family
Times
Old Age
New Ages
New Orders
Ordered
World
New
"Make Me King"
"As We Move"
Towards a "NWO"
Story
Battle
Prepare
Treatment
Royalty
New Aged Order
Places

Directions
Movements
Rules
Succeeds
Provides
Wealth
Abundance
Necessities
War
Living
Ruling
Strong
Loud
Silent
Proud
Big
Content
Product
Source
Provision
Transparent
Motionless
Motioning
Crowds
Personifying
Strongest
King
New
Order
Every
One
Thing
Not
As Is
Isn't
Worth

Value
Rightness
Noteworthy
Practiced
Valuable
Against
Wills
Protagonist
War
Legion
Faction
Spiritual
Leadership
Foundation
Physical
Emotional
Intellectuals
Mistakes
Errors
Wrongs
Brains
Brawn
Know
Young
Prides
Values
Oldest
Aged
Order
Sciences
Physicality
Directions
Medications
Bandages
Syringes
War's

Peaceful
Times

The Road Less Traveled On-

That Has Made All The Difference!

Know
Sense
Awareness
Crowds
Biggest
Lives
Supporting
Holding
Building-Up
Partings
Eventually
Diverging
Challenges
Out Measurable
Willpowers
Parting
Ways
Separated
Differenced
Wayward
Directionally
Found
Support
Travels
Ending
Stopping
Point
Separated
Differenced

Wayward
Directionally
Found
Support
Travels
Ending
Stopping
Point
Separating
Learnable
Took
Less
More
Roads

THE ROADS TO WWIII!

Firstly
Chosen
Arranged
Presumably
Guessed
Calculate
Know
Hire
Concerned
Ability
Trajectory
Target
Miserable
Calculated
Misleading
Found
Traded
Disclosed

Numbered
Calculated
Measured
Christian
Unbelievable
Faithful
Righteous
Considered
Valueless
Hard
High
Climb
Discovery
Agreeableness
Valuable

THE HARD WAY – TO WWIII?

Antisocial
Unbelieving
Weakest
Strongly
Kinds
Prophetic
Knights
Darkened
Founded
Different
Divisions
Directed
Roads
Whole
Intersections
Lighted
Chosen

Left
Right
Wrongful
Directly
Alone
Woods
Divided
Destination
Unknowing
Evaluated
Choice
Proud
Rewarded
Paths
Straight
Unconformity
Story
Tale
Endings
Nuclear
Atomic
Weapons
America
Divisions
Straight
Forwards
Divided
Resumed
Repeated
Proclaim
Resounded
Valued
Limitless
Holocaust's
Desecration
Tragedy

Found-Out
Dead
Silence

THE WWIII STAGE!

Tanks
Guns
Soldiers
Ammunition
Infantry
Slaughtering
Killing
Graves
Losing
Rest
Death
Burials
Topics
Strangers
Personalities
Lives
Dreamt
Condemned
Lifelessness
Trail
Human
Directed
Founded
Saved
Dead
Alive
Harden
Souls
Ditched

Found Again
Rediscovered
Remade
Resounded
Limitless
Find
Lived
Became
Questioned
Unknown
War
Friends
Foes

What Repeats History?
Is WW3 Relived Again?

New Order
New World Order
New Aged Order
Ordered
Repeated
Aged Thrice
Tripled War
One World
Two Sides
Divided
Humungous
Separated
Allied
Joined
Good Sided
Evil
Opponents

Homeliness
Joint
Twice
Friends
Divided
Deaths
Orders
Divine
Wicked
Twofold
One World
Another World
Both "New" Ordered
Worldviews
Heroes
Villains
Gone
Won
USA
Alive
Dead
Found
Strength
Deaths
Godspeed!
Government
New World Order
Antichrist's WWIII
End Times
Biblical American's WW3
Governing Bodies
Dead USA Party
USA
Endings
Deaths
All of It

Dead and Gone
The End Is Near
History of Wars
Third War of Worlds
World War Three
Under USA Law
Be an American
Try WW3 American
Jesus Christ In WWIII
God the Father In Ending
The Church In Apocalypse
World War of NWO
History of WWIII to WW3!
The Military Genius of USA's!
The WWIII
The End of Creation in WW3!
The End of USA!
War Times in A.C.'S USA
The Loss of All Lives
The Lasting Endings Of Itself –
WW3 Intellect Is In Secret Societies
American Plans From Old Retold War Lives
Remembering The History's Warred Figures
Costing The Price To Pay, To Lives Whom Lost
    Comparing Presidential Books And War
  Books, Of WWIII

    Life And Death, To Wins Over WW3

    To Try To Win! WW3!

  USA

WW3
"A.C."
USA'S Antichrist One World
Sold to World Democracy

Bought By Final Offers
First One-World Government
Shadow Laws
One World Government
NOA
America's First Democracy
            The   Entire   USA
      All USA Followers of World

The New World Order
The Free World
Leader of Free World
Antichrist America
WWIII However, Is Dead at USA Ending?

      My Lesson In World War III –

      The New World Order, Government!

Force of Real Law
Public Forces of Legalities
Private Function From NWO'S WWIII
The Party of the First Democracy
The Whole Worldwide Followers
Every Citizen Is Counted Included
Public Offices Serve Citizens
Governing Officials Served N.W.O.'S WW3
Private Functions Relive WWII
The Government Is One-World-Order
The Followers Are From All Worlds
The Democracy Is Public Decisions
The A.C. Of One Man Is Represented
The Beast's Followers are False People
Heaven Fell Apart When A.C.'S WWIII Is

Democracy   Is   Alive   In   USA
Follower's Party Agrees With New USA
Order

The USA's N.W.O. Hires One-World Government
WW3 Presidential Office
Hired Office of WWIII – Govern World Democracy
1-World Government/ NWO
Antichristian Life Head Towards Presidential
   Endings

"THE THIRD WORLD WAR!"

   What Riley Does In Wars, In How He Hires
The Office, Of Intention To Will Into Power!

   What Words, Are Written That Wills, Wars
Into Power? The President Of The United
States!

RILEY MILLER OF AMERICA!
√XOΩ

From Riley Parker Miller –

A Bible Topic in My Holy Bible –

'PRIDE PROMOTES STRIFE'

James 4 – 6
In NKJV Holy Bible

JAMES 4 – 1

"Where do wars and fights come
From among you?
Do, they not come from your
Desires for *pleasure*,
That war in your members?

4 – 2

You lust and do not have.
You murder and covet and cannot obtain.
You fight, and war.
Yet you do not have because you do not ask.
4 – 3

You ask and do not receive,
Because you ask amiss,
That you may spend it on your pleasures.

4 – 4

Adulterers and Adulteresses!

Do you not know that friendship

With the world, is enmity with God?

Whoever therefore wants to be a

Friend of the world makes himself,

An enemy of God.
4 – 5

Or do you think that the Scriptures,

SAYS IN VAIN, "THE SPIRIT WHO

Dwells in us yearns jealously?"
4 – 6

But   He   gives   more   grace.
Therefore He says:

"God resists the proud,
But gives grace to the humble."

TITUS 2 – 14

Who gave Himself for us,
That He might redeem us
From every lawless deed
And purify for Himself
His own special people,
Zealous for good works.

From-
The Epistle of James

Jesus Christ In Bible's Verses
The Holy Bible
THE NEW KING JAMES
VERSION!

The Writing Codex, Of The Book's
Protection From Biblical Codex, Came From
Out Of The Reader's Writing of Words, Desired
To Be From, What Is In The Intelligent
Designed Of The System!

From The Ways Of Man! From What Is In,
This Written Style, On The Styles, Of The
Books, From The Presidential Elected – "Third
War Office"! The book's message, Therein
Lives Another Life, In The – "New World
Order!"

Riley Miller Is The Approved Contributor,
To This Book, As The Churched Elicit Prophet!

Treasury, is in Heaven, how you will, and
show, to store up wealth. But, on this earth,
therein will be showed, up to the top; certain
people's lives. They, can be nurtured, onto
showing the design of the world! They, are the
architects. They are, "The Freemasons!" This –
is their intelligent design world.

A Book Solely By – "Riley Parker Miller!" √

THE HISTORY'S BOOKS PROVEN TRUE IN LAW OF LANDS

I Wrote Books, The Books Of the History In Loving And Living The Everything In Life, To Its Greatest Form – "Books Of The Best Quality". I, Never In Intelligence Had To Fail, And From Good Teaching, Comes Knowledge, Inyo Easy Books, Of Greatest, And Biggest, Then Boldest, And Also Smartest, Books – I Will Into Power! The Intelligence On Books, As For The Easiest To Read, Into Is The Library's History, Lives From All Around, The State Of Texas, Into – The Top Of The World!

Front Lines, of war people!
God's Omega's Codex!
The "As Smart Man" Business Deal!

THE BOOK WRITES ITSELF!

Highest Dragon Order

A Series of Riley Miller's Books